YOUR
HOROSCOPE
2018

♌

LEO

YOUR PERSONAL HOROSCOPE 2018

LEO

23rd July–23rd August

igloobooks

Published in 2017
by Igloo Books Ltd
Cottage Farm
Sywell
NN6 0BJ
www.igloobooks.com

Produced for Igloo Books by Foulsham Publishing Ltd, The Old Barrel Store,
Drayman's Lane, Marlow, Bucks SL7 2FF, England

FIR003 0717
2 4 6 8 10 9 7 5 3 1
ISBN: 978-1-78670-881-6

This is an abridged version of material originally published
in Old Moore's Horoscope and Astral Diary.

Cover design by Charles Wood-Penn
Edited by Bobby Newlyn-Jones

Printed and manufactured in China

CONTENTS

INTRODUCTION

Your Personal Horoscopes have been specifically created to allow you to get the most from astrological patterns and the way they have a bearing on not only your zodiac sign, but nuances within it. Using the diary section of the book you can read about the influences and possibilities of each and every day of the year. It will be possible for you to see when you are likely to be cheerful and happy or those times when your nature is in retreat and you will be more circumspect. The diary will help to give you a feel for the specific 'cycles' of astrology and the way they can subtly change your day-to-day life. For example, when you see the sign ☿, this means that the planet Mercury is retrograde at that time. Retrograde means it appears to be running backwards through the zodiac. Such a happening has a significant effect on communication skills, but this is only one small aspect of how the Personal Horoscope can help you.

With Your Personal Horoscope the story doesn't end with the diary pages. It includes simple ways for you to work out the zodiac sign the Moon occupied at the time of your birth, and what this means for your personality. In addition, if you know the time of day you were born, it is possible to discover your Ascendant, yet another important guide to your personal make-up and potential.

Many readers are interested in relationships and in knowing how well they get on with people of other astrological signs. You might also be interested in the way you appear to very different sorts of individuals. If you are such a person, the section on Venus will be of particular interest. Despite the rapidly changing position of this planet, you can work out your Venus sign, and learn what bearing it will have on your life.

Using Your Personal Horoscope you can travel on one of the most fascinating and rewarding journeys that anyone can take – the journey to a better realisation of self.

THE ESSENCE
OF LEO

Exploring the Personality of Leo the Lion

(23RD JULY – 23RD AUGUST)

What's in a sign?

What really sets you apart from the herd is your naturally cheerful tendencies and your ability to display a noble and very brave face to the world at large. Leos are big people, no matter what their physical size may be and it is clear that you could never be an 'also-ran'. Quite the reverse is usually the case because you are at the forefront of many ventures, ideas and enterprises.

Being a Leo brings quite a few responsibilities. For example, people tend to look up to you, which means you have to be on your best behaviour for a lot of the time. Not that this prevents you from showing a slightly mischievous face to the world on a regular basis. You are not given to worrying too much because you generally know how to get yourself out of any sort of difficulty with ease. It's true that you tend to face problems head-on – a natural extension of your rather courageous temperament. Sometimes this can get you into unnecessary scrapes, as can your tendency to pit yourself against the forces of nature, or social groups that you feel to be absolutely wrong in their intentions or objectives.

As a Leo you do recognise that you have a responsibility to others, particularly those types who are shyer than you, or individuals who just don't have the ability to look after themselves. With a smile and a shrug you are inclined to put a protecting arm around the whole world. In effect you are the perfect big brother or sister and take pride in the position you tend to gain in society. In a work sense you are capable and can very easily find yourself in a situation of responsibility. You don't worry about this and can make a fine executive in almost any profession. There's no doubt though that you are naturally best placed at the head of things.

It's true that you are inclined to do too much and that your levels of energy are far from inexhaustible. However, it's a love of life that counts for the most in your case, and nothing is going to prevent you from being the happy, sunny, freewheeling soul that represents the sign of Leo at its very best.

Leo resources

Your ruling planet is the Sun, the source of all heat, light and therefore life on the Earth. The Sun is fundamental to our very existence, and its primary importance at the centre of things is reflected in your nature. Unlike your brother sign, Aries, you display your Fire-sign tendencies in a more controlled manner and without the need to dominate to such a great extent. All the same your natural position is at the head of things and this is reflected in the resources you draw from the zodiac.

One of your greatest gifts is a natural tendency to look confident, even on those occasions when you might be quaking inside. It's amazing what a difference this makes because it more or less ensures that others will trust you and tend to follow your lead. Once they do you rise to the occasion in an admirable way because you don't want to let your followers down. In almost any situation that life could present, you will quite naturally take charge, and those around you are invariably happy that it should be so.

Most Leos are capable in a practical as well as a theoretical way but a hands-on approach probably works best. Leo leads from the front, which means having to keep fit and healthy. This is vital, but like the lion that your sign represents you can get rather lethargic and flabby if you don't keep in shape. Also like the lion you do have a tendency to appear lazy on occasions, but only usually when things are already running smoothly around you.

The professions chosen by Leos are many and varied. It isn't really the subject matter that is important, merely your ability to make an impression. At work, as well as in social situations, you can shine like the very Sun that rules you. Usually well liked and respected, you are in a position to utilise the popularity that comes your way in order to feather your own nest, as well as those of people around you. Domestically speaking you have a great love of home and family, though you might tend to stifle those you love a little on occasions.

Beneath the surface

'What really makes me tick?' A fair question, and one that members of many zodiac signs are constantly inclined to ask themselves – but not you. The fact is that you are not the deepest thinker around. This is not to suggest that you don't have lofty ideals or a very sound moral base to your behaviour. The reason that you probably are not one of life's natural philosophers is because you are a 'doer'. In the time it takes others to mull over any given situation you will have sorted it out and moved on to the next task. However, this is a natural skill that can be honed to perfection and depends in part on getting yourself interested in the first place.

Your boredom threshold tends to be quite low and you would soon feel fatigued if you were forced to remain in situations which meant doing the same thing time and time again. Your driving, sometimes impatient mentality does demand change, and you can become irritable and out of sorts if you don't find it.

Are you as confident as you often appear to be? The answer to that one has to be yes. The fact is that you quite often fail to bear in mind the possibility of failure. Of course this means that you are more disappointed than most when things do go wrong, but your very conviction often leads to success. Once you do get down in the dumps however, you can be a very sorry picture indeed. Fortunately, you have the mental and spiritual reserves to pick yourself up fairly quickly and to push forward once again.

In matters of love you are probably more reserved than you give the impression of being. All the same you know how to deal with relationships – that is until you start acting like a lion again. The over-protective quality of your animal sign is always a danger, and one that you need to control. Perhaps here we find the Achilles heel of Leo. It is quite common for you to experience a sense of jealousy, a fact that would make you more possessive than usual. You have to remember that it's fine to love, but impossible to 'own' another individual.

In the main you offer the world an exterior smile that reflects your genuine inner state. Truthfulness shows on your face, and is usually felt in your heart in equal proportion.

Making the best of yourself

To feel good and to make the right sort of impression, you have to look good too. Nobody goes to the safari park to see a moth-eaten lion. You can dress cheaply, but you have to cut a dash in some way. Drab colours definitely don't suit your personality, with bright oranges and yellows being the most favoured – a reflection of your Sun rulership. Once you are properly attired you tend to move forward positively through life. Most Leos are quite attractive people, mainly because the honesty, frankness and genuine courage of your personality has a habit of finding its way to the surface.

There is one line of Kipling's famous poem 'If' that springs to mind as an object lesson for Leo, this being 'And yet don't look too good, nor talk too wise'. It is quite possible for you to go over the top in your enthusiasm and even courage isn't same thing as foolhardiness. A little humility can go a long way, as can a determination to learn from people who know better than you do. Constantly knocking your head against the same brick wall isn't very productive, and can sometimes be avoided by simply showing a willingness to take advice. And it isn't as if people are unwilling to lend a hand. The Leo subjects who achieve the most in life have learned how to co-operate, though without feeling that they are having to relinquish the leading position in life that is so important to them.

In order for you truly to make the best of yourself you also need to be fit. Leos are inclined to have some problems associated with the heart and the circulatory system, so you need to exercise regularly and to avoid the sort of constant stress that can lead to longer-term health difficulties. To most Leos laughter is the best tonic of all.

The impressions you give

If we could all genuinely see ourselves as others see us, how much easier would be our interaction with the world at large? Yours may not be the most intuitive sign of the zodiac but you are perceptive enough to know when you are giving the right impression. If this fact is sometimes obscured it is at least easy for you to monitor when things are not going right. In turn this should result in a slight modification of your own personality to take account of circumstances.

If you have any specific problem in this direction it stems from the fact that you are not a natural philosopher. Doing is far more important than thinking to you, a truism that can sometimes be your downfall. More attention to detail and a better appraisal of others allow you to offer a much better impression of yourself.

Most people already find you sunny, warm, frank, free, delightfully outspoken and very brave. All you have to do to achieve real success is to build on the qualities you already possess and to make allowance for the fact that the world is full of individuals. You can't browbeat others into liking you, even though popularity is important to you. There will always be people who don't take to your personality and there really isn't much you can do about the situation.

A great advantage for you is that it isn't difficult for you to appear to know what you are talking about, even when you don't. You can gain extra skills on the way and should use the very real magnetism of your personality both to help the world and to improve your own situation. Few people would find you easy either to dismiss or to forget, which can be another very definite advantage in life.

A sense of proportion is sometimes important, as well as a defined purpose in your statements and actions. All in all you have most of the components that allow you to be popular. Build on these and your true Leo worth will be there for all to see.

The way forward

No sign of the zodiac typifies its planetary ruler more than your own sign of Leo. When you smile, the Sun comes out and your laughter is so infectious that even the hardest-hearted types would be likely to smile themselves. Add to this the fact that you typify the statement 'fools rush in where angels fear to tread' and you have a formidable combination at your disposal. It might be the case that you fail to take account of some of your actions, but a good-humoured and intelligent attitude to life also allows you to get out of scrapes as easily as you get into them.

Cultivate your tendency to stick up for the underdog and don't get yourself into a position in life that means you constantly have to pay lip service to people who clearly don't know what they are doing. You can't stand incompetence, arrogance, cruelty or oppression. Of course this is a fine attitude, but you can't put the world right on your own, so once again co-operation proves to be the key to success.

In a career sense you need to be doing something that constantly stretches you. Your boredom threshold is not high and with constant tedium can come a worrisome streak and a tendency to health difficulties. Variety in work is the spice of your life, together with an active and useful social life, which is also vitally important. In matters of love you are sincere and ardent, though with a tendency towards being a little too possessive. Allowing others the freedom to go their own way means finding more happiness yourself and lifts the noble qualities of your nature to new heights. Leos are still more likely than people from other zodiac signs to find one important relationship in life and to stick with it. Part of the reason for this state of affairs is that you have a horror of failure and will persist, even when others fall by the wayside.

You may not be creative in the generally accepted sense of the word but you have a good eye for colour and enjoy cheerful surroundings. Practical and capable, you won't need to call on the services of experts too often, since Leos generally don't shy away from DIY chores.

Diet is vitally important because as a Leo you are inclined to put on weight readily. Exercise helps here and is something you revel in anyway. Use your natural talents to the full, defend the weak and fight oppressors and you can't go far wrong in your life. Most important of all, keep smiling. You are tremendous fun to have around.

LEO ON THE CUSP

Astrological profiles are altered for those people born at either the beginning or the end of a zodiac sign, or, more properly, on the cusps of a sign. In the case of Leo this would be on the 23rd of July and for two or three days after, and similarly at the end of the sign, probably from the 21st to the 23rd of August.

The Cancer Cusp – July 23rd to July 25th

You tend to take life at a slower pace than Leo when taken on its own. You are more sensitive and quieter by nature, with slightly less drive and enthusiasm and a less dynamic disposition. With a creative and generally aspiring nature, you draw from Leo the fearless qualities that are typical of the sign, but these only tend to show on those occasions when you feel very strongly about things. There is quite a contradiction between these two signs and therefore you have a tendency to show very different faces in different circumstances. This fact makes you slightly awkward to predict and you often shock people as a result. Just when the world thinks it has you pigeon-holed, off you go at a tangent, perplexing your relatives and friends all over again. Family members are very important to you and when your aspiring and lofty qualities show most it is often on their behalf. In matters of love you tend to be very loyal, and have the ability to mix very well with others, enjoying cheerful and original people as part of your social circle.

One area that needs particular attention is your health. Although generally more robust than you probably give yourself credit for, you get through a tremendous amount of nervous energy, much more than others may realise. You need to watch your diet very carefully and to avoid acidic foods, which can upset your stomach. Apart from this, however, you are virtually indestructible and have the capacity to work long and hard to achieve your objectives.

At work you do your best to be adaptable and are very good at managing others. The natural frustrations of Leo, when faced with opposition, are less accented in your case. You have the ability to get on well and should make a mark for yourself when happy with your lot. Few would find you overbearing or bossy, although at times you seem to lack some of the natural Leo confidence. Most important of all though – you are kind, generous, trusting and very good to know.

The Virgo Cusp – August 21st to August 23rd

Perhaps the greatest difficulty for people born under the influence of this cusp is in making themselves understood. You probably think that you are the least complicated person in the world, but that isn't the way others see you. Your nature is full of contradictions. On the one hand you are fanatically tidy, and yet you can work in a state of almost total chaos; you love to travel and yet, deep inside, you are a home bird; and you talk a great deal, but often with quiet confidence. To disentangle all these contradictions is as difficult for you as it is for anyone else, and so you may often not reach the level of self-confidence that you deserve.

You have most of the positive qualities associated with the zodiac sign of Leo and your lofty, aspiring, sunny disposition is usually well accepted. Beneath this, however, is a quiet and contemplative person, who needs moments alone to synthesise the many happenings in a busy life. Usually physically robust, you do tend to worry more than is good for you, frequently about matters that are not particularly important. Meditation suits you well, particularly the kind that has a physical aspect, as this satisfies your Leo qualities, too. With a nervous system that varies from day to day, it is important for you to be sure that you achieve the level of relaxation that is vital to your Virgoan qualities. For you this could be anything between a crossword puzzle and two weeks on a cruise ship. In social settings you enjoy a degree of variety and can manage quite well with new people, even though you often tend to stick to people with whom you are familiar.

It's always important for you to keep an open mind and you shouldn't allow negative thoughts to build up. Keeping busy makes sense, as long as you don't continually choose to burn the candle at both ends. The people who know you the best do find you difficult to understand, but they are inclined to love you all the more for that. The most important character trait for you to cultivate is optimism because the more cheerful you remain regarding the future, the greater is the effort you expound upon it.

LEO AND ITS ASCENDANTS

The nature of every individual on the planet is composed of the rich variety of zodiac signs and planetary positions that were present at the time of their birth. Your Sun sign, which in your case is Leo, is one of the many factors when it comes to assessing the unique person you are. Probably the most important consideration, other than your Sun sign, is to establish the zodiac sign that was rising over the eastern horizon at the time that you were born. This is your Ascending or Rising sign. Most popular astrology fails to take account of the Ascendant, and yet its importance remains with you from the very moment of your birth, through every day of your life. The Ascendant is evident in the way you approach the world, and so, when meeting a person for the first time, it is this astrological influence that you are most likely to notice first. Our Ascending sign essentially represents what we appear to be, while the Sun sign is what we feel inside ourselves.

The Ascendant also has the potential for modifying our overall nature. For example, if you were born at a time of day when Leo was passing over the eastern horizon (this would be around the time of dawn) then you would be classed as a double Leo. As such, you would typify this zodiac sign, both internally and in your dealings with others. However, if your Ascendant sign turned out to be a Water sign, such as Pisces, there would be a profound alteration of nature, away from the expected qualities of Leo.

One of the reasons why popular astrology often ignores the Ascendant is that it has always been rather difficult to establish. We have found a way to make this possible by devising an easy-to-use table, which you will find on page 157 of this book. Using this, you can establish your Ascendant sign at a glance. You will need to know your rough time of birth, then it is simply a case of following the instructions.

For those readers who have no idea of their time of birth it might be worth allowing a good friend, or perhaps your partner, to read through the section that follows this introduction. Someone who deals with you on a regular basis may easily discover your Ascending sign, even though you could have some difficulty establishing it for yourself. A good understanding of this component of your nature is essential if you want to be aware of that 'other person' who is responsible for the way you make contact with the world at large. Your Sun sign, Ascendant sign, and the other pointers in this book will, together, allow you a far better understanding of what makes you tick as an individual. Peeling back the different layers of your astrological make-up can be an enlightening experience, and the Ascendant may represent one of the most important layers of all.

Leo with Leo Ascendant

This is a breathless combination! The fact is that you are a go-getter of the first order, and there is virtually nothing in life that would prevent you from getting what you want. The problem here is that once you have it, you probably want something else. All in all you could end up like a dog chasing its own tail and so the first advice is to slow down and enjoy the journey a little more. Not that all of this makes you any less likeable, or indispensable, to a whole host of people. You smile much more often than you scowl and you won't make heavy weather of problems that would rock others back on their heels.

You are rather materialistic, and ultimate success probably means more to you than it should, but you can easily stop on your hectic journey to take note of those who have fallen by the wayside and give them a helping hand. If all that power is used for the good of humanity you might even become a living saint, except for the fact that you would be too busy to accept the honour. Be careful that you don't weigh yourself down with so many responsibilities that you fail to notice your progress, and travel as much as you can because this will certainly broaden your mind. Most people find you very attractive and fun to have around.

Leo with Virgo Ascendant

Here we have cheerfulness allied to efficiency, which can be a very positive combination for most of the time. With all the sense of honour, justice and bravery of the Leo subject, Virgo adds better staying power through tedious situations and offers you a slightly more serious view of life than we would expect from the Lion alone. In almost any situation you can keep going until you get to your chosen destination and you also find the time to reach out to the people who need your unique nature the most. Few would deny your kindness, though you can attract a little envy because it seems as though yours is the sort of personality that everyone else wants.

Most people born with this combination have a radiant smile and will do their utmost to think situations through carefully. If there is any tendency to be foolhardy, it is carefully masked beneath a covering of Virgoan common sense. Family matters are dealt with efficiently and with great love. Some might see you as close one moment and distant the next. The truth is that you are always on the go and have a thousand different things to think about, all at the same time. On the whole your presence is noticed, and you may represent the most loyal friend of them all.

Leo with Libra Ascendant

Libra brings slightly more flexibility to the fixed quality of the Leo nature. On the whole you do not represent a picture that is so very different from other versions of the Lion, though you find more time to smile, enjoy changing your mind a great deal more and have a greater number of casual friends. Few would find you proud or haughty and you retain the common touch that can be so important when it comes to getting on in life generally. At work you like to do something that brings variety, and would probably soon tire of doing the same task over and over again. Many of you are teachers, for you have patience, allied to a stubborn core. This can be an indispensable combination on occasions and is part of the reason for the material success that many folk with this combination achieve.

It isn't often that you get down in the dumps, as there is generally something more important around the next corner and you love the cut and thrust of everyday life. You always manage to stay young at heart, no matter what your age might be, and you revel in the company of interesting and stimulating types. Maybe you should try harder to concentrate on one thing at once and also strive to retain a serious opinion for more than ten minutes at a time, although Leo does help to control any flighty tendencies which show up.

Leo with Scorpio Ascendant

A Leo with intensity, that is what you are. You are committed to good causes and would argue the hind leg off a donkey in defence of your many ideals. If you are not out there saving the planet you could just be at home in the bath, thinking up the next way to save humanity from its own worst excesses. In your own life, although you love little luxuries, you are sparing and frugal, yet generous as can be to those you take to. It's a fact that you don't like everyone and of course the same is true in reverse. It might be easier for you to understand why you dislike others than to appreciate the reverse side of the coin, for your pride can be badly dented on occasions. Scorpio brings a tendency to have down spells, though the fact that Leo is also strongly represented in your nature should prevent them from becoming a regular part of your life.

It is important for you to learn how to forgive and forget, and there isn't much point in bearing a grudge because you are basically too noble to do so. If something goes wrong, kiss the situation goodbye and get on with the next interesting adventure, of which there are many in your life. Stop-start situations sometimes get in the way but there are plenty of people around who would be only too willing to lend a helping hand.

Leo with Sagittarius Ascendant

Above and beyond anything else you are naturally funny, and this is an aspect of your nature that will bring you intact through a whole series of problems that you manage to create for yourself. Chatty, witty, charming, kind and loving, you personify the best qualities of both these signs, whilst also retaining the Fire-sign ability to keep going, long after the rest of the party has gone home to bed. Being great fun to have around, you attract friends in the way that a magnet attracts iron filings. Many of these will be casual connections but there will always be a nucleus of deep, abiding attachments that may stay around you for most of your life.

You don't often suffer from fatigue, but on those occasions when you do there is ample reason to stay still for a while and simply take stock of situations. Routines are not your thing and you like to fill your life with variety. It's important to do certain things right, however, and staying power is something that comes with age, assisted by the fixed quality of Leo. Few would lock horns with you in an argument, which you always have to win. In a way you are a natural debator but you can sometimes carry things too far if you are up against a worthy opponent. Confidence is not lacking and you go with ease through situations that would cause many people to give up.

Leo with Capricorn Ascendant

What really sets you apart is your endless patience and determination to get where you want to go, no matter how long it takes you to do so. On the way there are many sub-plots in your life and a wealth of entertaining situations to keep you amused. Probably somewhat quieter than the average Leo, you still have the capacity to be the life and soul of the party on those occasions when it suits you to be so. Energy, when allied to persistence, is a powerful commodity and you have a great need to take on causes of one sort or another. Probably at your best when defending the rights of the oppressed, you take the protecting qualities of Leo to greater heights than almost anyone else who is touched by the idealistic and regal qualities of the sign. If arguments come into your life, you deal with them quickly and, in the main, wisely. Like most Capricorn types, you take to a few individuals who will play a part in your life for years on end.

Being a good family type, your partner and children are extremely important and you will lavish the same patience, determination and ultimate success on their behalf that you do when dealing with more remote situations. The fact is that you do not know any other way to behave and you are at your best when there is some mountain to climb.

Leo with Aquarius Ascendant

All associations with Aquarius bring originality, and you are no exception. You aspire to do your best most of the time, but manage to achieve your objectives in an infinitely amusing and entertaining way. Not that you set out to do so, because if you are an actor on the stage of life, it seems as though you are a natural one. There is nothing remotely pretentious about your breezy personality or your ability to occupy the centre of any stage. This analogy is quite appropriate because you probably like the theatre. Being in any situation when reality is suspended for a while suits you down to the ground, and in any case you may regularly ask yourself if you even recognise what reality is. Always asking questions, both of yourself and of the world at large, you soldier on relentlessly, though not to the exclusion of having a good time on the way.

Keeping to tried and tested paths is not your way. You are a natural trail-blazer who is full of good ideas and who has the energy to put them into practice. You care deeply for the people who play an important part in your life, but are wise enough to allow them the space they need in order to develop their own personalities along the way. Most people like you, many love you, and one or two think that you are the best thing since sliced bread.

Leo with Pisces Ascendant

You are a very sensitive soul, on occasions too much so for your own good. However, there is no better advocate for the rights of humanity than you, and you constantly do what you can to support the downtrodden and oppressed. Good causes are your thing and there are likely to be many in your life. You will probably find yourself pushed to the front of almost any enterprise of which you are a part because, despite the deeper qualities of Pisces, you are a natural leader. Even on those occasions when it feels as though you lack confidence, you manage to muddle through somehow, and your smile is as broad as the day. Few sign combinations are more loved than this one, mainly because you do not have a malicious bone in your body and will readily forgive and forget, which the Lion on its own often will not.

Although you are capable of acting on impulse, you do so from a deep sense of moral conviction, so that most of your endeavours are designed to suit other people too. They recognise this fact, and will push a great deal of support back in your direction. Even when you come across troubles in your life you manage to find ways to sort them out, and will invariably find something new to smile about on the way. Your sensitivity rating is massive and you can easily be moved to tears.

Leo with Aries Ascendant

Here we come upon a situation in which Leo is allied with another Fire sign. This creates a character that could appear to be typically Aries at first sight and in many ways it is, though there are subtle differences that should not be ignored. Although you have the standard Aries ability for getting things done, many of the tasks you do undertake will be for and on behalf of others. You can be proud, and on some occasions even haughty, and yet you are also regal in your bearing and honest to the point of absurdity. Nobody could doubt your sincerity, and you have the soul of a poet combined with the bravery of a lion.

All of this is good, but it makes you rather difficult to approach, unless the person in question has first adopted a crouching and subservient attitude. Not that you would wish them to do so. It's simply that the impression you give and the motivation that underpins it are two quite different things. You are greatly respected, and in the case of those individuals who know your real nature, you are also deeply loved. But life would be much simpler if you didn't always have to fight the wars that those around you are happy to start. Relaxation is a word you don't really understand and you would be doing yourself a favour if you looked it up in a dictionary.

Leo with Taurus Ascendant

Oh dear, this can be rather a hedonistic combination. The trouble is that Taurus tends to have a great sense of what looks and feels right, whilst Leo, being a Cat, is inclined to preen itself on almost any occasion. The combination tends towards self-love, which is all too likely for someone who is perfect. But don't be too dispirited about these facts, because there is a great deal going for you in other ways. For a start you have one of the warmest hearts to be found anywhere, and you are so brave that others marvel at the courage you display. The mountains that you climb may not be of the large, rocky sort, but you manage to find plenty of pinnacles to scale all the same, and you invariably get to the top.

Routines might bore you a little more than would be the case with Taurus alone, but you don't mind being alone. Why should you? You are probably the nicest person you know! Thus if you were ever to be cast up on a deserted island you would people the place all on your own, and there would never be any crime, untidiness or arguments. Problems only arise when other people are involved. However, in social settings you are charming, good to know and full of ideas that really have legs. You preserve your youth well into middle age but at base you can tend to worry more than is good for you.

Leo with Gemini Ascendant

Many Gemini people think about doing great things, whilst those who enjoy a Leo Sun do much more than simply think. You have the intrepid qualities of Gemini, but you always keep a sense of humour and are especially good to be around. Bold and quite fearless, you are inclined to go where nobody has gone before, no matter if this is into a precarious business venture or up a mountain that has not been previously climbed. It is people such as you who first explored the world, and you love to know what lies around the next corner and over the far hill.

Kind and loving, you are especially loyal to your friends and would do almost anything on their behalf. As a result they show the greatest concern for you too. However, there are times when the Cat walks alone, and you are probably better at being on your own than would often be the case for the typical Gemini subject. In many way you are fairly self-contained and don't tend to get bored too much unless you are forced to do the same things time and time again. You have a great sense of fun, could talk to just about anyone and usually greet the world with a big smile.

Leo with Cancer Ascendant

This can be a very fortunate combination, for when seen at its best it brings all the concern and the natural caring qualities of Cancer, allied to the more dynamic and very brave face of Leo. Somehow there is a great deal of visible energy here but it manifests itself in a way that always shows a concern for the world at large. No matter what charitable works are going on in your district, it is likely that you will be involved in one way or another, and you relish the cut and thrust of life much more than the retiring side of Cancer would seem to do. You are quite capable of walking alone and don't really need the company of others for large chunks of the average day. However, when you are in social situations you fare very well and can usually be observed with a smile on your face.

Conversationally speaking you have sound, considered opinions and often represent the voice of steady wisdom when faced with a situation that calls for arbitration. In fact you will often be put in this situation and there is more than one politician and union representative who shares this undeniably powerful zodiac combination. Like all those associated with the sign of Cancer you love to travel and can make a meal out of your journeys, with brave, intrepid Leo lending a hand in the planning and the doing.

THE MOON AND THE PART IT PLAYS IN YOUR LIFE

In astrology the Moon is probably the single most important heavenly body after the Sun. Its unique position, as partner to the Earth on its journey around the solar system, means that the Moon appears to pass through the signs of the zodiac extremely quickly. The zodiac position of the Moon at the time of your birth plays a great part in personal character and is especially significant in the build-up of your emotional nature.

Your Own Moon Sign

Discovering the position of the Moon at the time of your birth has always been notoriously difficult because tracking the complex zodiac positions of the Moon is not easy. This process has been reduced to three simple stages with our Lunar Tables. A breakdown of the Moon's zodiac positions can be found from page 35 onwards, so that once you know what your Moon Sign is, you can see what part this plays in the overall build-up of your personal character.

If you follow the instructions on the next page you will soon be able to work out exactly what zodiac sign the Moon occupied on the day that you were born and you can then go on to compare the reading for this position with those of your Sun sign and your Ascendant. It is partly the comparison between these three important positions that goes towards making you the unique individual you are.

HOW TO DISCOVER YOUR MOON SIGN

This is a three-stage process. You may need a pen and a piece of paper but if you follow the instructions below the process should only take a minute or so.

STAGE 1 First of all you need to know the Moon Age at the time of your birth. If you look at Moon Table 1, on page 33, you will find all the years between 1920 and 2018 down the left side. Find the year of your birth and then trace across to the right to the month of your birth. Where the two intersect you will find a number. This is the date of the New Moon in the month that you were born. You now need to count forward the number of days between the New Moon and your own birthday. For example, if the New Moon in the month of your birth was shown as being the 6th and you were born on the 20th, your Moon Age Day would be 14. If the New Moon in the month of your birth came after your birthday, you need to count forward from the New Moon in the previous month. Whatever the result, jot this number down so that you do not forget it.

STAGE 2 Take a look at Moon Table 2 on page 34. Down the left hand column look for the date of your birth. Now trace across to the month of your birth. Where the two meet you will find a letter. Copy this letter down alongside your Moon Age Day.

STAGE 3 Moon Table 3 on page 34 will supply you with the zodiac sign the Moon occupied on the day of your birth. Look for your Moon Age Day down the left hand column and then for the letter you found in Stage 2. Where the two converge you will find a zodiac sign and this is the sign occupied by the Moon on the day that you were born.

Your Zodiac Moon Sign Explained

You will find a profile of all zodiac Moon Signs on pages 35 to 38, showing in yet another way how astrology helps to make you into the individual that you are. In each daily entry of the Astral Diary you can find the zodiac position of the Moon for every day of the year. This also allows you to discover your lunar birthdays. Since the Moon passes through all the signs of the zodiac in about a month, you can expect something like twelve lunar birthdays each year. At these times you are likely to be emotionally steady and able to make the sort of decisions that have real, lasting value.

MOON TABLE 1

YEAR	JUN	JUL	AUG	YEAR	JUN	JUL	AUG	YEAR	JUN	JUL	AUG
1920	16	15	14	1953	11	11	9	1986	7	7	5
1921	6	5	3	1954	1/30	29	28	1987	26	25	24
1922	25	24	22	1955	20	19	17	1988	14	13	12
1923	14	14	12	1956	8	8	6	1989	3	3	1/31
1924	2	2/31	30	1957	27	27	25	1990	22	22	20
1925	21	20	19	1958	17	16	15	1991	11	11	9
1926	10	9	8	1959	6	6	4	1992	1/30	29	28
1927	29	28	27	1960	24	24	22	1993	20	19	17
1928	18	17	16	1961	13	12	11	1994	9	8	7
1929	7	6	5	1962	2	1/31	30	1995	27	27	26
1930	26	25	24	1963	21	20	19	1996	17	15	14
1931	16	15	13	1964	10	9	7	1997	5	4	3
1932	4	3	2/31	1965	29	28	26	1998	24	23	22
1933	23	22	21	1966	18	17	16	1999	13	13	11
1934	12	11	10	1967	7	7	5	2000	2	1/31	29
1935	1/30	30	29	1968	26	25	24	2001	21	20	19
1936	19	18	17	1969	14	13	12	2002	10	9	8
1937	8	8	6	1970	4	4	2	2003	29	28	27
1938	27	27	25	1971	22	22	20	2004	16	16	15
1939	17	16	15	1972	11	11	9	2005	6	6	4
1940	6	5	4	1973	1/30	29	28	2006	26	25	23
1941	24	24	22	1974	20	19	17	2007	15	15	13
1942	13	13	12	1975	9	9	7	2008	4	3	1/31
1943	2	2	1/30	1976	27	27	25	2009	23	22	20
1944	20	20	18	1977	16	16	14	2010	12	12	10
1945	10	9	8	1978	5	5	4	2011	2	2/31	29
1946	29	28	26	1979	24	24	22	2012	19	19	17
1947	18	17	16	1980	13	12	11	2013	8	7	6
1948	7	6	5	1981	2	1/31	29	2014	27	25	24
1949	26	25	24	1982	21	20	19	2015	17	16	15
1950	15	15	13	1983	11	10	8	2016	4	4	2
1951	4	4	2	1984	29	28	26	2017	24	23	22
1952	22	22	20	1985	18	17	16	2018	13	13	11

33

TABLE 2   *MOON TABLE 3*

DAY	JUL	AUG	M/D	R	S	T	U	V	W	X
1	R	U	0	CA	CA	LE	LE	LE	LE	VI
2	R	U	1	CA	LE	LE	LE	VI	VI	VI
3	S	V	2	LE	LE	LE	VI	VI	VI	LI
4	S	V	3	LE	LE	VI	VI	VI	LI	LI
5	S	V	4	LE	VI	VI	LI	LI	LI	LI
6	S	V	5	VI	VI	LI	LI	LI	SC	SC
7	S	V	6	VI	LI	LI	LI	SC	SC	SC
8	S	V	7	LI	LI	LI	SC	SC	SA	SA
9	S	V	8	LI	LI	SC	SC	SC	SA	SA
10	S	V	9	SC	SC	SC	SA	SA	SA	SA
11	S	V	10	SC	SC	SA	SA	SA	CP	CP
12	S	V	11	SA	SA	SA	CP	CP	CP	CP
13	T	V	12	SA	SA	SA	CP	CP	AQ	AQ
14	T	W	13	SA	SA	CP	CP	CP	AQ	AQ
15	T	W	14	CP	CP	CP	AQ	AQ	AQ	PI
16	T	W	15	CP	CP	AQ	AQ	AQ	PI	PI
17	T	W	16	AQ	AQ	AQ	AQ	PI	PI	PI
18	T	W	17	AQ	AQ	AQ	PI	PI	PI	AR
19	T	W	18	AQ	AQ	PI	PI	PI	AR	AR
20	T	W	19	PI	PI	PI	PI	AR	AR	AR
21	T	W	20	PI	PI	AR	AR	AR	TA	TA
22	T	W	21	PI	AR	AR	AR	TA	TA	TA
23	T	W	22	AR	AR	AR	TA	TA	TA	GE
24	U	X	23	AR	AR	TA	TA	TA	GE	GE
25	U	X	24	AR	TA	TA	TA	GE	GE	GE
26	U	X	25	TA	TA	GE	GE	GE	CA	CA
27	U	X	26	TA	GE	GE	GE	CA	CA	CA
28	U	X	27	GE	GE	GE	CA	CA	CA	LE
29	U	X	28	GE	GE	CA	CA	CA	LE	LE
30	U	X	29	GE	CA	CA	CA	LE	LE	LE
31	U	X								

AR = Aries, TA = Taurus, GE = Gemini, CA = Cancer, LE = Leo, VI = Virgo,
LI = Libra, SC = Scorpio, SA = Sagittarius, CP = Capricorn, AQ = Aquarius, PI = Pisces

MOON SIGNS

Moon in Aries

You have a strong imagination, courage, determination and a desire to do things in your own way and forge your own path through life.

Originality is a key attribute; you are seldom stuck for ideas although your mind is changeable and you could take the time to focus on individual tasks. Often quick-tempered, you take orders from few people and live life at a fast pace. Avoid health problems by taking regular time out for rest and relaxation.

Emotionally, it is important that you talk to those you are closest to and work out your true feelings. Once you discover that people are there to help, there is less necessity for you to do everything yourself.

Moon in Taurus

The Moon in Taurus gives you a courteous and friendly manner, which means you are likely to have many friends.

The good things in life mean a lot to you, as Taurus is an Earth sign that delights in experiences which please the senses. Hence you are probably a lover of good food and drink, which may in turn mean you need to keep an eye on the bathroom scales, especially as looking good is also important to you.

Emotionally you are fairly stable and you stick by your own standards. Taureans do not respond well to change. Intuition also plays an important part in your life.

Moon in Gemini

You have a warm-hearted character, sympathetic and eager to help others. At times reserved, you can also be articulate and chatty: this is part of the paradox of Gemini, which always brings duplicity to the nature. You are interested in current affairs, have a good intellect, and are good company and likely to have many friends. Most of your friends have a high opinion of you and would be ready to defend you should the need arise. However, this is usually unnecessary, as you are quite capable of defending yourself in any verbal confrontation.

Travel is important to your inquisitive mind and you find intellectual stimulus in mixing with people from different cultures. You also gain much from reading, writing and the arts but you do need plenty of rest and relaxation in order to avoid fatigue.

Moon in Cancer

The Moon in Cancer at the time of birth is a fortunate position as Cancer is the Moon's natural home. This means that the qualities of compassion and understanding given by the Moon are especially enhanced in your nature, and you are friendly and sociable and cope well with emotional pressures. You cherish home and family life, and happily do the domestic tasks. Your surroundings are important to you and you hate squalor and filth. You are likely to have a love of music and poetry.

Your basic character, although at times changeable like the Moon itself, depends on symmetry. You aim to make your surroundings comfortable and harmonious, for yourself and those close to you.

Moon in Leo

The best qualities of the Moon and Leo come together to make you warm-hearted, fair, ambitious and self-confident. With good organisational abilities, you invariably rise to a position of responsibility in your chosen career. This is fortunate as you don't enjoy being an 'also-ran' and would rather be an important part of a small organisation than a menial in a large one.

You should be lucky in love, and happy, provided you put in the effort to make a comfortable home for yourself and those close to you. It is likely that you will have a love of pleasure, sport, music and literature. Life brings you many rewards, most of them as a direct result of your own efforts, although you may be luckier than average and ready to make the best of any situation.

Moon in Virgo

You are endowed with good mental abilities and a keen receptive memory, but you are never ostentatious or pretentious. Naturally quite reserved, you still have many friends, especially of the opposite sex. Marital relationships must be discussed carefully and worked at so that they remain harmonious, as personal attachments can be a problem if you do not give them your full attention.

Talented and persevering, you possess artistic qualities and are a good homemaker. Earning your honours through genuine merit, you work long and hard towards your objectives but show little pride in your achievements. Many short journeys will be undertaken in your life.

Moon in Libra

With the Moon in Libra you are naturally popular and make friends easily. People like you, probably more than you realise, you bring fun to a party and are a natural diplomat. For all its good points, Libra is not the most stable of astrological signs and, as a result, your emotions can be a little unstable too. Therefore, although the Moon in Libra is said to be good for love and marriage, your Sun sign and Rising sign will have an important effect on your emotional and loving qualities.

You must remember to relate to others in your decision-making. Co-operation is crucial because Libra represents the 'balance' of life that can only be achieved through harmonious relationships. Conformity is not easy for you because Libra, an Air sign, likes its independence.

Moon in Scorpio

Some people might call you pushy. In fact, all you really want to do is to live life to the full and protect yourself and your family from the pressures of life. Take care to avoid giving the impression of being sarcastic or impulsive and use your energies wisely and constructively.

You have great courage and you invariably achieve your goals by force of personality and sheer effort. You are fond of mystery and are good at predicting the outcome of situations and events. Travel experiences can be beneficial to you.

You may experience problems if you do not take time to examine your motives in a relationship, and also if you allow jealousy, always a feature of Scorpio, to cloud your judgement.

Moon in Sagittarius

The Moon in Sagittarius helps to make you a generous individual with humanitarian qualities and a kind heart. Restlessness may be intrinsic as your mind is seldom still. Perhaps because of this, you have a need for change that could lead you to several major moves during your adult life. You are not afraid to stand your ground when you know your judgement is right, you speak directly and have good intuition.

At work you are quick, efficient and versatile and so you make an ideal employee. You need work to be intellectually demanding and do not enjoy tedious routines.

In relationships, you anger quickly if faced with stupidity or deception, though you are just as quick to forgive and forget. Emotionally, there are times when your heart rules your head.

Moon in Capricorn

The Moon in Capricorn makes you popular and likely to come into the public eye in some way. The watery Moon is not entirely comfortable in the Earth sign of Capricorn and this may lead to some difficulties in the early years of life. An initial lack of creative ability and indecision must be overcome before the true qualities of patience and perseverance inherent in Capricorn can show through.

You have good administrative ability and are a capable worker, and if you are careful you can accumulate wealth. But you must be cautious and take professional advice in partnerships, as you are open to deception. You may be interested in social or welfare work, which suit your organisational skills and sympathy for others.

Moon in Aquarius

The Moon in Aquarius makes you an active and agreeable person with a friendly, easy-going nature. Sympathetic to the needs of others, you flourish in a laid-back atmosphere. You are broad-minded, fair and open to suggestion, although sometimes you have an unconventional quality which others can find hard to understand.

You are interested in the strange and curious, and in old articles and places. You enjoy trips to these places and gain much from them. Political, scientific and educational work interests you and you might choose a career in science or technology.

Money-wise, you make gains through innovation and concentration and Lunar Aquarians often tackle more than one job at a time. In love you are kind and honest.

Moon in Pisces

You have a kind, sympathetic nature, somewhat retiring at times, but you always take account of others' feelings and help when you can.

Personal relationships may be problematic, but as life goes on you can learn from your experiences and develop a better understanding of yourself and the world around you.

You have a fondness for travel, appreciate beauty and harmony and hate disorder and strife. You may be fond of literature and would make a good writer or speaker yourself. You have a creative imagination and may come across as an incurable romantic. You have strong intuition, maybe bordering on a mediumistic quality, which sets you apart from the mass. You may not be rich in cash terms, but your personal gifts are worth more than gold.

LEO IN LOVE

Discover how compatible in love you are with people from the same and other signs of the zodiac. Five stars equals a match made in heaven!

Leo meets Leo

More of a mutual appreciation society than a relationship, this is a promising match. Leo is kind, considerate, lofty, idealistic and brave, all qualities which are mirrored by a Leo partner. Both Lions will be determined in their ambitions, recognise the importance of the family and share a mutual love in all areas of their lives. Furthermore, Leo loves to be loved and so will give and receive it in equal amounts. There won't be many arguments but when there are – watch out! Star rating: *****

Leo meets Virgo

There is a chance for this couple, but it won't be trouble-free. Leo and Virgo view life very differently: Virgo is of a serious nature, struggling to relate to Leo's relentless optimism and cheerfulness, and even finding it annoying. Leo, meanwhile, may find Virgo stodgy, sometimes dark, and uninspiring. The saving grace comes through communication – Leo knows how to make Virgo talk, which is what it needs. If this pair find happiness, though, it may be a case of opposites attract! Star rating: ***

Leo meets Libra

The biggest drawback here is likely to be in the issue of commitment. Leo knows everything about constancy and faithfulness, a lesson which, sadly, Libra needs to learn. Librans are easy-going and diplomatic, qualities which are useful when Leo is on the war-path. This couple should be compatible on a personal level and any problems tend to relate to the different way in which these signs deal with outside factors. With good will and an open mind, it can work out well enough. Star rating: ***

Leo meets Scorpio

Stand back and watch the sparks fly! Scorpio has the deep sensitivity of a Water sign but it is also partially ruled by Fire planet Mars, from which it draws a great power that Leo will find difficult. Leo loves to take charge and really hates to feel psychologically undermined, which is Scorpio's stock-in-trade. Scorpio may find Leo's ideals a little shallow, which will be upsetting to the Lion. Anything is possible, but this possibility is rather slimmer than most. Star rating: **

Leo meets Sagittarius

An excellent match, as Leo and Sagittarius have so much in common. Their general approach to life is very similar, although as they are both Fire signs they can clash impressively! Sagittarius is shallower and more flippant than Leo likes to think of itself, and the Archer will be the one taking emotional chances. Sagittarius has met its match in the Lion's den, as brave Leo won't be outdone by anyone. Financially, they will either be very wealthy or struggling, and family life may be chaotic. Problems, like joys, are handled jointly – and that leads to happiness. Star rating: *****

Leo meets Capricorn

Despite promising appearances, this match often fails to thrive. Capricorn focuses on long-term objectives and, like Leo, is very practical. Both signs are capable of attaining success after a great struggle, which while requiring effort, gives them a mutual goal. But when life is easier, the cracks begin to show. Capricorn can be too serious for Leo, and the couple share few ideals. Leo loves luxury, Capricorn seeks austerity. Leo is warm but Capricorn seems cold and wintry in comparison. Both have many good points, but they don't seem to fire each other off properly. Star rating: **

Leo meets Aquarius

The problem here is that Aquarius doesn't 'think' in the general sense of the word, it 'knows'. Leo, on the other hand, is more practical and relies more on logical reasoning, and consequently it doesn't understand Aquarius very well. Aquarians can also appear slightly frosty in their appreciation of others and this, too, will eventually annoy Leo. This is a good match for a business partnership because Aquarius is astute, while Leo is brave, but personally the prognosis is less promising. Tolerance, understanding and forbearance are all needed to make this work. Star rating: **

Leo meets Pisces

Pisces always needs to understand others, which makes Leo feel warm and loved, while Leo sees, to its delight, that Pisces needs to be protected and taken care of. Pisceans are often lacking in self-confidence, which is something Leo has to spare, and happily it is often infectious. Pisces' inevitable cares are swept away on a tide of Leonine cheerfulness. This couple's home would be cheerful, and full of love which is beneficial to all family members. This is not a meeting of minds, but rather an understanding and appreciation of differences. Star rating: ****

Leo meets Aries

Stand by for action and make sure that the house is sound-proof! Leo is a lofty idealist and there is always likely to be friction when two Fire signs meet. To compensate, there is much mutual admiration, together with a desire to please. Where there are shared incentives, the prognosis is good but it's important not to let little irritations blow up. Both signs want to have their own way and this is a sure cause of trouble. There might not be much patience here, but there is plenty of action. Star rating: *****

Leo meets Taurus

Here we find a generally successful pairing, which frequently leads to an enduring relationship. Taurus needs stimulation which Leo is happy to offer, while Leo responds well to the Bull's sense of order. The essence of the relationship is balance, but it may be achieved with wild swings of the scales on the way, so don't expect a quiet life, though this pair will enjoy a reconciliation after an argument! Material success is probable and, as both like children, a family is likely. Star rating: ***

Leo meets Gemini

There can be problems here, but Gemini is adaptable enough to overcome many of them. Leo is a go-getter and might sometimes rail against Gemini's flighty tendencies, while Gemini's mental disorganisation can undermine Leo's practicality. However, Leo is cheerful and enjoys Gemini's jokey, flippant qualities. At times of personal intimacy, the two signs should be compatible. Leo and Gemini share very high ideals, but Leo will stick at them for longer. Patience is needed on both sides for the relationship to develop. Star rating: ***

Leo meets Cancer

This relationship will usually be directed by dominant Leo more towards its own needs than Cancer's. However, the Crab will willingly play second fiddle to more progressive and bossy types as it is deeply emotional and naturally supportive. Leo is bright, caring, magnanimous and protective and so, as long as it isn't over-assertive, this could be a good match. On the surface, Cancer appears the more conventional of the two, but Leo will discover, to its delight, that underneath it can be unusual and quirky. Star rating: ****

VENUS:
THE PLANET OF LOVE

If you look up at the sky around sunset or sunrise you will often see Venus in close attendance to the Sun. It is arguably one of the most beautiful sights of all and there is little wonder that historically it became associated with the goddess of love. But although Venus does play an important part in the way you view love and in the way others see you romantically, this is only one of the spheres of influence that it enjoys in your overall character.

Venus has a part to play in the more cultured side of your life and has much to do with your appreciation of art, literature, music and general creativity. Even the way you look is responsive to the part of the zodiac that Venus occupied at the start of your life, though this fact is also down to your Sun sign and Ascending sign. If, at the time you were born, Venus occupied one of the more gregarious zodiac signs, you will be more likely to wear your heart on your sleeve, as well as to be more attracted to entertainment, social gatherings and good company. If on the other hand Venus occupied a quiet zodiac sign at the time of your birth, you would tend to be more retiring and less willing to shine in public situations.

It's good to know what part the planet Venus plays in your life for it can have a great bearing on the way you appear to the rest of the world and since we all have to mix with others, you can learn to make the very best of what Venus has to offer you.

One of the great complications in the past has always been trying to establish exactly what zodiac position Venus enjoyed when you were born because the planet is notoriously difficult to track. However, we have solved that problem by creating a table that is exclusive to your Sun sign, which you will find on the following page.

Establishing your Venus sign could not be easier. Just look up the year of your birth on the following page and you will see a sign of the zodiac. This was the sign that Venus occupied in the period covered by your sign in that year. If Venus occupied more than one sign during the period, this is indicated by the date on which the sign changed, and the name of the new sign. For instance, if you were born in 1970, Venus was in Virgo until the 8th August, after which time it was in Libra. If you were born before 8th August your Venus sign is Virgo, if you were born on or after 8th August, your Venus sign is Libra. Once you have established the position of Venus at the time of your birth, you can then look in the pages which follow to see how this has a bearing on your life as a whole.

1920 LEO / 12.8 VIRGO
1921 GEMINI / 6.8 CANCER
1922 VIRGO / 11.8 LIBRA
1923 CANCER / 4.8 LEO
1924 GEMINI / 25.7 CANCER
1925 LEO / 28.7 VIRGO
1926 LEO / 24.7 VIRGO /
   18.8 LIBRA
1927 VIRGO
1928 LEO / 12.8 VIRGO
1929 GEMINI / 5.8 CANCER
1930 VIRGO / 10.8 LIBRA
1931 CANCER / 3.8 LEO
1932 GEMINI / 28.7 CANCER
1933 LEO / 27.7 VIRGO
1934 LEO / 23.7 VIRGO /
   17.8 LIBRA
1935 VIRGO
1936 LEO / 11.8 VIRGO
1937 GEMINI / 5.8 CANCER
1938 VIRGO / 10.8 LIBRA
1939 CANCER / 3.8 LEO
1940 GEMINI / 1.8 CANCER
1941 LEO / 27.7 VIRGO
1942 LEO / 23.7 VIRGO /
   17.8 LIBRA
1943 VIRGO
1944 LEO / 11.8 VIRGO
1945 GEMINI / 5.8 CANCER
1946 VIRGO / 9.8 LIBRA
1947 CANCER / 2.8 LEO
1948 GEMINI / 3.8 CANCER
1949 LEO / 26.7 VIRGO
1950 LEO / 23.7 VIRGO /
   16.8 LIBRA
1951 VIRGO
1952 LEO / 10.8 VIRGO
1953 GEMINI / 4.8 CANCER
1954 VIRGO / 9.8 LIBRA
1955 CANCER / 1.8 LEO
1956 GEMINI / 4.8 CANCER
1957 LEO / 26.7 VIRGO
1958 VIRGO / 16.8 LIBRA
1959 VIRGO
1960 LEO / 9.8 VIRGO
1961 GEMINI / 4.8 CANCER
1962 VIRGO / 9.8 LIBRA
1963 CANCER / 1.8 LEO
1964 GEMINI / 5.8 CANCER
1965 LEO / 25.7 VIRGO
1966 VIRGO / 16.8 LIBRA
1967 VIRGO
1968 LEO / 9.8 VIRGO
1969 GEMINI / 4.8 CANCER

1970 VIRGO / 8.8 LIBRA
1971 CANCER / 31.7 LEO
1972 GEMINI / 5.8 CANCER
1973 LEO / 25.7 VIRGO
1974 VIRGO / 15.8 LIBRA
1975 VIRGO
1976 LEO / 9.8 VIRGO
1977 GEMINI / 3.8 CANCER
1978 VIRGO / 8.8 LIBRA
1979 CANCER / 31.7 LEO
1980 GEMINI / 6.8 CANCER
1981 LEO / 24.7 VIRGO
1982 VIRGO / 15.8 LIBRA
1983 VIRGO
1984 LEO / 8.8 VIRGO
1985 GEMINI / 3.8 CANCER
1986 VIRGO / 7.8 LIBRA
1987 CANCER / 30.7 LEO
1988 GEMINI / 6.8 CANCER
1989 LEO / 24.7 VIRGO
1990 VIRGO / 14.8 LIBRA
1991 VIRGO / 22.8 LEO
1992 LEO / 8.8 VIRGO
1993 GEMINI / 2.8 CANCER
1994 VIRGO / 7.8 LIBRA
1995 CANCER / 30.7 LEO
1996 GEMINI / 7.8 CANCER
1997 LEO / 24.7 VIRGO
1998 VIRGO / 14.8 LIBRA
1999 VIRGO / 22.8 LEO
2000 LEO / 8.8 VIRGO
2001 GEMINI / 1.8 CANCER
2002 VIRGO / 8.8 LIBRA
2003 CANCER / 30.7 LEO
2004 GEMINI / 7.8 CANCER
2005 LEO / 24.7 VIRGO
2006 VIRGO / 14.8 LIBRA
2007 VIRGO / 22.8 LEO
2008 LEO / 8.8 VIRGO
2009 GEMINI / 1.8 CANCER
2010 VIRGO / 8.8 LIBRA
2011 CANCER / 30.7 LEO
2012 GEMINI / 7.8 CANCER
2013 LEO / 24.7 VIRGO
2014 VIRGO / 14.8 LIBRA
2015 VIRGO / 22.8 LEO
2016 LEO / 6.8 VIRGO
2017 GEMINI / 1.8 CANCER
2018 VIRGO / 8.8 LIBRA

VENUS THROUGH THE ZODIAC SIGNS

Venus in Aries

Amongst other things, the position of Venus in Aries indicates a fondness for travel, music and all creative pursuits. Your nature tends to be affectionate and you would try not to create confusion or difficulty for others if it could be avoided. Many people with this planetary position have a great love of the theatre, and mental stimulation is of the greatest importance. Early romantic attachments are common with Venus in Aries, so it is very important to establish a genuine sense of romantic continuity. Early marriage is not recommended, especially if it is based on sympathy. You may give your heart a little too readily on occasions.

Venus in Taurus

You are capable of very deep feelings and your emotions tend to last for a very long time. This makes you a trusting partner and lover, whose constancy is second to none. In life you are precise and careful and always try to do things the right way. Although this means an ordered life, which you are comfortable with, it can also lead you to be rather too fussy for your own good. Despite your pleasant nature, you are very fixed in your opinions and quite able to speak your mind. Others are attracted to you and historical astrologers always quoted this position of Venus as being very fortunate in terms of marriage. However, if you find yourself involved in a failed relationship, it could take you a long time to trust again.

Venus in Gemini

As with all associations related to Gemini, you tend to be quite versatile, anxious for change and intelligent in your dealings with the world at large. You may gain money from more than one source but you are equally good at spending it. There is an inference here that you are a good communicator, via either the written or the spoken word, and you love to be in the company of interesting people. Always on the look-out for culture, you may also be very fond of music, and love to indulge the curious and cultured side of your nature. In romance you tend to have more than one relationship and could find yourself associated with someone who has previously been a friend or even a distant relative.

Venus in Cancer

You often stay close to home because you are very fond of family and enjoy many of your most treasured moments when you are with those you love. Being naturally sympathetic, you will always do anything you can to support those around you, even people you hardly know at all. This charitable side of your nature is your most noticeable trait and is one of the reasons why others are naturally so fond of you. Being receptive and in some cases even psychic, you can see through to the soul of most of those with whom you come into contact. You may not commence too many romantic attachments but when you do give your heart, it tends to be unconditionally.

Venus in Leo

It must become quickly obvious to almost anyone you meet that you are kind, sympathetic and yet determined enough to stand up for anyone or anything that is truly important to you. Bright and sunny, you warm the world with your natural enthusiasm and would rarely do anything to hurt those around you, or at least not intentionally. In romance you are ardent and sincere, though some may find your style just a little overpowering. Gains come through your contacts with other people and this could be especially true with regard to romance, for love and money often come hand in hand for those who were born with Venus in Leo. People claim to understand you, though you are more complex than you seem.

Venus in Virgo

Your nature could well be fairly quiet no matter what your Sun sign might be, though this fact often manifests itself as an inner peace and would not prevent you from being basically sociable. Some delays and even the odd disappointment in love cannot be ruled out with this planetary position, though it's a fact that you will usually find the happiness you look for in the end. Catapulting yourself into romantic entanglements that you know to be rather ill-advised is not sensible, and it would be better to wait before you committed yourself exclusively to any one person. It is the essence of your nature to serve the world at large and through doing so it is possible that you will attract money at some stage in your life.

Venus in Libra

Venus is very comfortable in Libra and bestows upon those people who have this planetary position a particular sort of kindness that is easy to recognise. This is a very good position for all sorts of friendships and also for romantic attachments that usually bring much joy into your life. Few individuals with Venus in Libra would avoid marriage and since you are capable of great depths of love, it is likely that you will find a contented personal life. You like to mix with people of integrity and intelligence but don't take kindly to scruffy surroundings or work that means getting your hands too dirty. Careful speculation, good business dealings and money through marriage all seem fairly likely.

Venus in Scorpio

You are quite open and tend to spend money quite freely, even on those occasions when you don't have very much. Although your intentions are always good, there are times when you get yourself in to the odd scrape and this can be particularly true when it comes to romance, which you may come to late or from a rather unexpected direction. Certainly you have the power to be happy and to make others contented on the way, but you find the odd stumbling block on your journey through life and it could seem that you have to work harder than those around you. As a result of this, you gain a much deeper understanding of the true value of personal happiness than many people ever do, and are likely to achieve true contentment in the end.

Venus in Sagittarius

You are lighthearted, cheerful and always able to see the funny side of any situation. These facts enhance your popularity, which is especially high with members of the opposite sex. You should never have to look too far to find romantic interest in your life, though it is just possible that you might be too willing to commit yourself before you are certain that the person in question is right for you. Part of the problem here extends to other areas of life too. The fact is that you like variety in everything and so can tire of situations that fail to offer it. All the same, if you choose wisely and learn to understand your restless side, then great happiness can be yours.

Venus in Capricorn

The most notable trait that comes from Venus in this position is that it makes you trustworthy and able to take on all sorts of responsibilities in life. People are instinctively fond of you and love you all the more because you are always ready to help those who are in any form of need. Social and business popularity can be yours and there is a magnetic quality to your nature that is particularly attractive in a romantic sense. Anyone who wants a partner for a lover, a spouse and a good friend too would almost certainly look in your direction. Constancy is the hallmark of your nature and unfaithfulness would go right against the grain. You might sometimes be a little too trusting.

Venus in Aquarius

This location of Venus offers a fondness for travel and a desire to try out something new at every possible opportunity. You are extremely easy to get along with and tend to have many friends from varied backgrounds, classes and inclinations. You like to live a distinct sort of life and gain a great deal from moving about, both in a career sense and with regard to your home. It is not out of the question that you could form a romantic attachment to someone who comes from far away or be attracted to a person of a distinctly artistic and original nature. What you cannot stand is jealousy, for you have friends of both sexes and would want to keep things that way.

Venus in Pisces

The first thing people tend to notice about you is your wonderful, warm smile. Being very charitable by nature you will do anything to help others, even if you don't know them well. Much of your life may be spent sorting out situations for other people, but it is very important to feel that you are living for yourself too. In the main, you remain cheerful, and tend to be quite attractive to members of the opposite sex. Where romantic attachments are concerned, you could be drawn to people who are significantly older or younger than yourself or to someone with a unique career or point of view. It might be best for you to avoid marrying whilst you are still very young.

LEO:
2017 DIARY PAGES

October

2017

1 SUNDAY
Moon Age Day 11   Moon Sign Aquarius

All of a sudden it seems as though the wind is taken out of your sails and if this is so you can blame the arrival of the lunar low. Don't be too quick to take on anything new and wait for a day or two before you embark on any sort of adventure. Take the chance on offer at the moment to get some real, solid rest.

2 MONDAY
Moon Age Day 12   Moon Sign Aquarius

Your options might seem somewhat limited right now but that is only because of the present position of the Moon. All the same it would be wise not to push your luck too much and to wait until tomorrow before you really get adventurous. In your mind at least you are very inventive and well able to plan ahead.

3 TUESDAY
Moon Age Day 13   Moon Sign Pisces

This is a good day for constructive career building and for planning ahead as far as your professional life is concerned. There could be a slight lull in romantic potential but that is probably because you are so busy doing other things. Try not to be too selective about jobs and sort out some of the less pleasant ones too.

4 WEDNESDAY
Moon Age Day 14   Moon Sign Pisces

The social contacts you have been making of late can be of great use to you right now. This will be especially true in professional situations. Don't be too surprised if you are sought out for special treatment from those in authority and make sure you show how pleased you are when someone close to home seeks your opinion, too.

5 THURSDAY
Moon Age Day 15   Moon Sign Aries

If there have been specific worries at the back of your mind you should discover that at least a few of them now disappear like the morning mist. Maybe you have worried them out of existence but it is far more likely that you were making too much of an issue of them in the first place. A feeling of significant relief could follow.

6 FRIDAY
Moon Age Day 16   Moon Sign Aries

The support you now receive from others should be stronger at the moment than has seemed to be the case for quite some time. Make use of this situation by relying on colleagues and good friends, whilst at the same time checking details and making certain that you are still fully in command of all situations yourself.

7 SATURDAY
Moon Age Day 17   Moon Sign Taurus

Today marks a slightly demanding period and a time during which you really do have to buckle down to something you don't relish too much. Once you get started there should be little or no problem but it's the thought of unsavoury jobs that makes you feel a little uneasy at the start of this weekend.

8 SUNDAY
Moon Age Day 18   Moon Sign Taurus

There is a great deal in your chart now about self-expression, leisure and pleasure. All you need in order to make today go with a real swing is a good dose of optimism – together with the support of like-minded friends. Personal attachments should be strengthening and family members actively seek your advice around now.

9 MONDAY
Moon Age Day 19   Moon Sign Taurus

Social pleasure can now be integrated into your overall plans for the week. This is a good time to mix business with pleasure and to get satisfaction from both. New friendships may begin this week and people in positions of authority may respond well to you. All in all, a positive period for Leo.

10 TUESDAY   *Moon Age Day 20   Moon Sign Gemini*

Your insightful and independent approach to life is both refreshing and useful. Not everyone seems to have your best interests at heart but you do have what it takes to turn situations to your advantage, no matter what others might think. You should be dreaming up new and revolutionary ways to do tedious jobs.

11 WEDNESDAY   *Moon Age Day 21   Moon Sign Gemini*

Right now you don't care too much for the superficial and tend to be taking a deep and thorough look at life. Whilst other graze the surface of situations you will get out your microscope if necessary in order to make certain that you understand things. This kind of care will pay dividends in the end, even if some people laugh at you now.

12 THURSDAY   *Moon Age Day 22   Moon Sign Cancer*

This is a time for approaching success rather than expecting to reach it. You could do worse than to take stock for the next couple of days, as the Moon moves through your solar twelfth house. You can afford to take most things at face value but there are some issues that will require a little intuition.

13 FRIDAY   *Moon Age Day 23   Moon Sign Cancer*

Right now it is important to take life one step at a time and to avoid being overwhelmed if everything seems to be happening at once. Do not bite off more than you can chew at work and when you are at home allow relatives or your partner to do something on your behalf. Today isn't the most energetic day of the month for you.

14 SATURDAY   *Moon Age Day 24   Moon Sign Leo*

The lunar high brings what is likely to be the most progressive phase of the month and offers you the chance to get ahead on a number of different fronts. Arrangements made today show you to be in a very dynamic and go-getting frame of mind. Those with whom you mix are now very envious of your charisma and potential success.

15 SUNDAY
Moon Age Day 25   Moon Sign Leo

Things continue in a very positive way and some situations seem to be turning to your advantage, even without you trying very hard. A combination of past effort and present certainty allows you to glide towards your objectives, whilst on the surface you appear to be the coolest and most collected person around.

16 MONDAY
Moon Age Day 26   Moon Sign Virgo

A boost comes along to your ability to relate to the world at large. It seems you are more understanding and a good deal more sympathetic than might sometimes be the case. It's quite unusual to find Leo so willing to listen to other points of view but there isn't any doubt that for the moment you will be putting yourself out for anyone.

17 TUESDAY
Moon Age Day 27   Moon Sign Virgo

In a professional sense you would now do especially well in any job that utilises your diplomatic skills. This is not something that could be said about Leo all the time but for now and for some days to come you could charm the very birds from the trees. People will be that much more approachable as a result and so benefits roll in.

18 WEDNESDAY
Moon Age Day 28   Moon Sign Libra

A good period comes along for all sorts of relationships. Most of your energy has recently been pushed out in the direction of the practical and professional world but under present trends you will be spending more time thinking about personal matters. It's hard to see how you could fail in love, especially if you concentrate on it.

19 THURSDAY
Moon Age Day 29   Moon Sign Libra

You may get a good deal of satisfaction from being helpful or sorting out things that confuse others but which are simplicity itself to you. Most of what you do is undertaken in an unassuming way and your present apparent humility makes you attractive to even more people. Watch your spending for the moment.

20 FRIDAY
Moon Age Day 0   Moon Sign Libra

Personal discussions could be inspirational and there is certainly mileage in talking things through, particularly at work. Advancement is likely for some in the very near future but you need to be on the ball if you are going to catch the gaze of people who have it in their power to improve your lot. Colleagues may not be too helpful.

21 SATURDAY
Moon Age Day 1   Moon Sign Scorpio

Rise to the challenge of addressing short-term goals as quickly as you can. This is not a day to let the grass grow under your feet and the sooner you get started, the better are the possibilities for later. When the practical side of life is out of the way you will probably want to curl up on the sofa with a good book or a television programme.

22 SUNDAY
Moon Age Day 2   Moon Sign Scorpio

You may be after achieving success by expanding your social contacts and this certainly is a fortunate time for mixing business with pleasure. New people come into your life at this time and one or two of them could turn out to be life-long friends. Analyse the personalities of those with whom you come into contact very carefully.

23 MONDAY
Moon Age Day 3   Moon Sign Sagittarius

At the start of a new working week it is clear that you have a great talent for invention and can think up new ways of doing old things all the time. Whether anyone will listen to your suggestions remains to be seen but in most situations it will be worth a try. Your powers of communication are very good now so get talking.

24 TUESDAY
Moon Age Day 4   Moon Sign Sagittarius

Your partner could prove to be quite demanding at the moment and this fact could inspire a few fireworks unless you use your diplomacy. There are some issues that simply are not worth arguing about and today will throw a few of these into the ring. What does it matter who is right or wrong? It's the ultimate results that count.

25 WEDNESDAY   *Moon Age Day 5*   *Moon Sign Sagittarius*

Put your best foot forward today and explore new ways of dealing with old situations. It's true there are some fairly awkward people about but you will deal with them quite easily. This is because you mix consideration with know-how and come up with solutions that suit everyone. These trends are Leo at its best and they are with you for some time.

26 THURSDAY   *Moon Age Day 6*   *Moon Sign Capricorn*

Any new and ingenious idea is grist to your mill today and you will be extremely inventive in most of your dealings with the world. You have been moving in exactly the right direction and some very positive vibes should be coming back at you. Just be careful that you don't push yourself a little too hard.

27 FRIDAY   *Moon Age Day 7*   *Moon Sign Capricorn*

At the present time you are a super-sensitive person with a great need to feel safe and secure. Right now you could easily take exception to anyone who seems to be trying to upset your world in any way and you will react strongly if you feel threatened. The only problem is that you may occasionally defend yourself before you are attacked.

28 SATURDAY   *Moon Age Day 8*   *Moon Sign Aquarius*

Shelve important decisions if you can or let a trusted colleague take some of the strain. You need thinking time and the lunar low offers you that possibility. This is certainly not the best day of the month to gamble in any way and where possible it would be best to keep your money firmly locked in your purse or wallet.

29 SUNDAY   *Moon Age Day 9*   *Moon Sign Aquarius*

Your expectations could still be rather too high but it's a fact that most people don't work at the weekend so if you are one of them you can at least find some time to relax. By tomorrow you should be right back on form and well able to cope with anything that comes along. Leo people hate to feel they are not in full control.

30 MONDAY *Moon Age Day 10   Moon Sign Pisces*

Getting ahead at work has a good deal to do with the way you approach people and it's fair to say that you have been kindness itself across the last couple of weeks. Of course this doesn't assure you of unbridled success because there are some people around who simply won't listen. More persuasion is needed in certain directions.

31 TUESDAY *Moon Age Day 11   Moon Sign Pisces*

You should find yourself in the best of company and this is a time for happy encounters, whether you are looking for them or not. You remain deeply romantic but you won't always say the right thing, no matter how hard you try. There are frustrations about today and you will simply have to work through them.

November 2017

1 WEDNESDAY *Moon Age Day 12 Moon Sign Pisces*

Professional developments should be on a roll today and you have what it takes to make a good impression on just about everyone you meet. Don't be fooled into thinking that someone knows better than you do about any aspect of your life because you are especially shrewd, calculating and in the know at present.

2 THURSDAY *Moon Age Day 13 Moon Sign Aries*

It looks as though under present trends you will enjoy the company of a wide range of different sorts of people. You show great charm and a willingness to take the other person's point of view on board a little more than would sometimes be the case. At work you may be finding new avenues for your existing talents.

3 FRIDAY *Moon Age Day 14 Moon Sign Aries*

You can glean some profound insights today and show yourself to be very astute and even quite psychic. In a practical sense you need to dump outmoded concepts or efforts that have proven themselves to be a waste of time. Don't chase rainbows that you know are going to disappear as soon as you approach them.

4 SATURDAY *Moon Age Day 15 Moon Sign Taurus*

Maybe you could afford to be just a little more ambitious and even manipulative at the moment. Of course you don't want to feel that you are manoeuvring people into positions that work to their disadvantage but this is not what you will be doing. Almost everything you undertake now has positive repercussions for others.

5 SUNDAY *Moon Age Day 16   Moon Sign Taurus*

Following the same general pattern that has been obvious for a while now you tend to break ties that are no longer of any use to you and will be making new friendships all the time. The potential for romance is good and especially so for Leos who are presently forming new attachments or formalising more casual ones.

6 MONDAY *Moon Age Day 17   Moon Sign Gemini*

Your inner drive is fully in gear and what you want more than anything at the moment is to feel that you are improving in every possible way. This might lead you to a desire to remodel yourself, perhaps through diet or health regimes. If so, proceed with caution. In time you can achieve anything but be steady.

7 TUESDAY *Moon Age Day 18   Moon Sign Gemini*

There could just be an intimate issue that is on your mind at the moment and if this is the case you ought to get it sorted out before you move on to other matters. There are some small surprises in store at present and though most of these will work to your advantage you do need to be in a position to respond to situations quickly.

8 WEDNESDAY *Moon Age Day 19   Moon Sign Cancer*

There is now the same powerful desire to get things done that typifies your zodiac sign. Any restrictions are out of the way and nothing will hold you back when you are certain of the direction you wish to take. Pay attention to what your partner or a good friend is saying. If you do, you could save yourself a lot of effort.

9 THURSDAY *Moon Age Day 20   Moon Sign Cancer*

A desire for personal freedom is now so strong within you that you would do almost anything to avoid feeling fettered. There is nothing at all odd about this as far as you are concerned. The fact is that Leo needs space and can soon get very frustrated and even ill if it is restricted to places or situations that feel wrong.

10 FRIDAY   *Moon Age Day 21   Moon Sign Leo*

You show yourself to be dynamic, keen to get ahead and more than happy to join in with like-minded people. This is Leo at its very best and is an excellent period in which to get things done. You thrive on competition and if you are involved in sporting activities today there is every chance that you will surpass yourself. However, stay focused.

11 SATURDAY   *Moon Age Day 22   Moon Sign Leo*

There is a beneficial period on the way as far as work is concerned but it is possible you will find it difficult to concentrate on necessary tasks today. This is because your mind is elsewhere and because you are dealing with ideas that you cannot put into practice just for the moment. Routines are a chore but they are important too.

12 SUNDAY   *Moon Age Day 23   Moon Sign Virgo*

This is a fascinating day to be out and about and should not be spent doing either boring or routine jobs. If your time is your own find some way to take a break, most rewardingly in the company of someone you love to be with. The evening could offer interesting social possibilities, as well as some new sort of diversion.

13 MONDAY   *Moon Age Day 24   Moon Sign Virgo*

You can apply your intuition to problem-solving today and should have a good deal of fun on the way. There are areas of your life that might need improving, or else things you want to address out there in the world as a whole. Whatever you turn your mind to at present is grist to the mill of your curiosity.

14 TUESDAY   *Moon Age Day 25   Moon Sign Libra*

You should be in for a happy phase at home and will be creating an especially caring and sharing sort of environment for yourself and your loved ones. The most pleasing moments you encounter today are likely to come along courtesy of family members and you show yourself to have more time than usual for domestic issues.

15 WEDNESDAY   *Moon Age Day 26   Moon Sign Libra*

A little positive thinking on your part could bring some very happy experiences and should allow you to work positively towards a longed-for objective in a personal sense. People are anxious to help you out at present and it is clear that you remain popular within almost any group. People look to you for guidance.

16 THURSDAY   *Moon Age Day 27   Moon Sign Libra*

Your emotional and romantic relationships tend to be far from reserved at the moment. When it comes to speaking your mind you are certainly not going to remain in the background and almost everyone you come across will notice your presence. There are times today when you feel king or queen of the world.

17 FRIDAY   *Moon Age Day 28   Moon Sign Scorpio*

Though there are some tricky decisions to be dealt with around this time there isn't any doubt that you are discriminating and very positive in your general outlook. One or two really awkward situations will be dealt with before you even realise the risks and as far as relationships are concerned it appears that you are on top form today.

18 SATURDAY   *Moon Age Day 0   Moon Sign Scorpio*

The social highlights are likely to continue and you certainly seem to be full of yourself under present planetary trends. Fortunately you will also be charming when in company and charismatic when it comes to new ventures. Practically everyone will want to follow your lead and even usually awkward people will fall in line.

19 SUNDAY   *Moon Age Day 1   Moon Sign Sagittarius*

If you are feeling emotionally pressured today this could be because you are simply taking on too much. It would be sensible to stop and rest for a while but that isn't the way for Leo. Instead of trying to do everything on your own it would be a distinct advantage for you to accept help from others. This, too, may be out of the question.

20 MONDAY *Moon Age Day 2   Moon Sign Sagittarius*

You seem to be in a Sherlock Holmes frame of mind at the beginning of this week because you want to know how everything works and will pit yourself against any awkward situation as a matter of course. There is just a slight possibility, though, that you will overlook specific issues that will be obvious to others.

21 TUESDAY *Moon Age Day 3   Moon Sign Sagittarius*

It doesn't appear that you are the best team player for the moment, mainly because you don't want to share the glory and will insist on doing practically everything your own way. Standing up for yourself seems more important than ever and there is a slight danger that you will be rather too forceful in your response to others.

22 WEDNESDAY *Moon Age Day 4   Moon Sign Capricorn*

You should concentrate now on reliable long-term plans and give up any thought of instant solutions or immediate gratification. It is likely that the warmer and more sympathetic side of your nature will begin to show again – much to the relief of colleagues and some friends. General good luck could be somewhat absent today.

23 THURSDAY *Moon Age Day 5   Moon Sign Capricorn*

Teamwork situations are your best avenue on this particular Thursday and this turns out to be the case whether you are at work or simply enjoying yourself at home. When other people make suggestions you are now more likely to listen and will gain a great deal from modifying the ideas of family members and contributing to their happiness.

24 FRIDAY *Moon Age Day 6   Moon Sign Aquarius*

You may be unable to take full control of certain issues today and will have little choice but to allow someone else to make the running. The lunar low saps your strength and prevents you from racing ahead in the way you have become used to doing. There is nothing else for it but to watch and wait, which will do you good.

25 SATURDAY   *Moon Age Day 7   Moon Sign Aquarius*

Progress will be slim at best but since this is the weekend it probably doesn't matter at all. You will doubtless be happiest at home just now and can gain greatly from the support and reassurance that comes from your partner and family members. Don't get hung up on pointless details today but spend time looking at the bigger picture.

26 SUNDAY   *Moon Age Day 8   Moon Sign Aquarius*

When concentrating on those things you have done many times before, you could appear to be almost super-human to colleagues or friends. The fact is that you are capable, have great staying power and will be at your best when faced with any challenge. Confidence is high and your abilities are not in doubt to anyone.

27 MONDAY   *Moon Age Day 9   Moon Sign Pisces*

The area of joint finance is under scrutiny – especially if you think that a business or life partner is not on the ball in terms of investments. This is not a good time to gamble with anyone's money and especially not your own. On occasion you could be rather too critical for your own good so do be willing to compromise more.

28 TUESDAY   *Moon Age Day 10   Moon Sign Pisces*

What a great period this is for widening your horizons and for showing the world at large how capable you can be. There could be the odd disappointment in store if not everyone comes up to the expectations you have had of them but you are also quite patient at present, which will help. When things do go wrong just start again.

29 WEDNESDAY   *Moon Age Day 11   Moon Sign Aries*

You won't have to look too far to find security and personal happiness at this stage of the year. It's true that family members can pose the odd problem for you but these are minor in nature and soon sorted out. Harmony should be evident at home and you will be turning your mind towards thoughts of the festive season that lies ahead.

30 THURSDAY   *Moon Age Day 12   Moon Sign Aries*

It's time for a few small indulgences and to treat yourself rather more than would usually be the case. In social situations you will be quite happy to hog the limelight and others will be pleased that you are taking centre-stage. Of course not everyone loves you but that's part of the penalty of being a Fire sign.

December 2017

1 FRIDAY
Moon Age Day 13   Moon Sign Taurus

It will probably only occur to you today that this is the first of December and so therefore Christmas is only a few short weeks away. Maybe that's a good thing because you are not the sort of person who does best by planning for things like holidays months ahead. Today should be steady and fruitful.

2 SATURDAY
Moon Age Day 14   Moon Sign Taurus

Your tongue and wit are both extremely sharp at present and whilst this is a very positive trend there is just a slight possibility that you could offer someone offence without realising you have done so. Maybe just a little more concern for the sensibilities of people in your vicinity is called for right now.

3 SUNDAY
☿ *Moon Age Day 15   Moon Sign Gemini*

Figures in positions of authority will be noticing you more than usual – not because you are sucking up to them but simply because you are making such a positive impression at the moment. As a result you could be marked out for special treatment. Confidence remains especially high for Leo people who are career specialists.

4 MONDAY
☿ *Moon Age Day 16   Moon Sign Gemini*

Today should see a boost to practical affairs and continues to work in your favour. If it seems you are somewhat short of cash you need to delve deep into your originality and to think up new ways to earn more. The upcoming Christmas season now becomes a serious issue in your mind – perhaps in some ways slightly belatedly.

5 TUESDAY ☿ *Moon Age Day 17 Moon Sign Cancer*

There is much to gain from all co-operative ventures at this time, particularly so in the case of Leos who are involved in business partnerships. Personal attachments are also well starred and it might be the magic of the season but you show yourself to be deeply romantic and more inclined to speak words of love.

6 WEDNESDAY ☿ *Moon Age Day 18 Moon Sign Cancer*

You now have quicker access to information that can easily be turned to your advantage. If you are involved in some inward battle, for example stopping smoking or trying to control your weight, keep up your efforts but at the same time avoid being quite as hard on yourself as might sometimes be the case.

7 THURSDAY ☿ *Moon Age Day 19 Moon Sign Leo*

Your thinking tends to be inspired and with the lunar high present you can put many of your most important thoughts into action. It's time to get busy and to show everyone who you are and what you are capable of doing. On the way you should encounter more than your fair share of good luck.

8 FRIDAY ☿ *Moon Age Day 20 Moon Sign Leo*

Most issues will be going your way, mainly because you are willing to take life by the scruff of the neck and shake it into what you want. There is a slightly ruthless streak about but as long as you look out for the good of others, as well as looking after your own interests, this shouldn't be much of a problem.

9 SATURDAY ☿ *Moon Age Day 21 Moon Sign Virgo*

You tend to be in a slightly excitable mood today and could easily be over-reacting to situations that would not normally move you much. Avoid arguing simply for the sake of doing so and whenever possible take the line of least resistance in discussions. If you shoot from the hip too much you will regret it later.

10 SUNDAY ☿ *Moon Age Day 22   Moon Sign Virgo*

You may find it easy to bend career situations to your own advantage and will be quite persuasive, even with those who are in overall authority. Things just seem to go your way, as indeed they will in the main. This is one of those periods during which Leo is on a roll, but be careful because things could change if your attention is lost.

11 MONDAY ☿ *Moon Age Day 23   Moon Sign Virgo*

You tend to be more and more outgoing as the days slip by and will certainly be in the limelight where social situations are concerned. For some reason your popularity is even higher now. It could be that you are presently encountering many different invitations and you will be loath to turn down any of them.

12 TUESDAY ☿ *Moon Age Day 24   Moon Sign Libra*

Your need for better communication and your desire to get out more combine to indicate a restless but potentially interesting time at hand. You want to get in touch with lots of people but the problem is that there are not enough hours in a day to achieve all your objectives. Patience Leo – patience!

13 WEDNESDAY ☿ *Moon Age Day 25   Moon Sign Libra*

You need more genuine fun and stimulating romance in your life at this time and the planets are likely to oblige. Entertaining others is as simple as encountering them in social situations or else inviting them to your home. Most people find you absolutely fascinating to have around and will be happy to tell you so.

14 THURSDAY ☿ *Moon Age Day 26   Moon Sign Scorpio*

Professional freedom could be more important than ever under present trends and you will be doing everything you can to strike out on your own and to get away from the plans of others that you see as being worthless. Stay open to new possibilities and stand by to fill in a gap if someone else falls sick or isn't equal to a specific task.

15 FRIDAY
☿ *Moon Age Day 27* *Moon Sign Scorpio*

There could hardly be a better time than this for getting out and seeing what is happening in your vicinity. The winter weather is closing in but that won't bother you in the slightest. On the contrary you are more than happy to dress up warmly and to make the best of your leisure hours out of doors. Romance looks secure and happy.

16 SATURDAY
☿ *Moon Age Day 28* *Moon Sign Scorpio*

If you have one problem to deal with at the moment it is likely to be that you are less than organised. This won't go down at all well because you love to have everything sorted and to be fully in command of your life. Soon enough you will be back on form but for the moment it might be necessary to simply relax and wait.

17 SUNDAY
☿ *Moon Age Day 29* *Moon Sign Sagittarius*

You should benefit from a more independent approach to life from now on and despite the fact that this is a Sunday your thoughts may well be on the changes you want to make at work. The build-up to Christmas will also be on your mind and there will probably be a number of family matters to get sorted before the big day.

18 MONDAY
☿ *Moon Age Day 0* *Moon Sign Sagittarius*

Perhaps you should choose today to get another breath of fresh air, both in a real and a figurative sense. Get out and see what is happening beyond the boundaries of your usual world and take a greater delight in the odd or unusual. There ought to be moments free to make your feelings known to loved ones, particularly your partner.

19 TUESDAY
☿ *Moon Age Day 1* *Moon Sign Capricorn*

This can be a fortunate period for you in both a professional and a personal sense. This period of December is one of the very best interludes for mixing business with pleasure – something that appeals to you and which leaves you feeling very satisfied. Not everyone will be on the ball so it's important to check and double-check matters.

20 WEDNESDAY ☿ *Moon Age Day 2   Moon Sign Capricorn*

Not only is today extremely expansive, it might also prove to be fairly expensive unless you have your wits about you. Don't make rash purchases until you have checked things out. Buying online or from catalogues might not be favourable for the moment but there are some good first-hand bargains if you spend time looking.

21 THURSDAY ☿ *Moon Age Day 3   Moon Sign Capricorn*

Although Christmas is generally a time for families and close friendships, Leo has the ability to use the social gatherings in order to further professional objectives. This could certainly be the case today, particularly since your cheerful and happy nature is making a favourable impression on so many potentially influential people.

22 FRIDAY ☿ *Moon Age Day 4   Moon Sign Aquarius*

You probably won't want to push yourself too hard today, or even leave your favourite chair much if you have any choice in the matter. The lunar low makes you contemplative and quite happy to sit on the riverbank of life for a while, watching the water flow by. This is not a time for prohibitive actions.

23 SATURDAY *Moon Age Day 5   Moon Sign Aquarius*

Practical setbacks are possible and when they come along all you can do is to deal with them one at a time. By tomorrow everything should look quite different, which is why it would be sensible to shelve certain jobs until later. If you don't you could find yourself having to repeat them later in any case.

24 SUNDAY *Moon Age Day 6   Moon Sign Pisces*

Christmas Eve ought to find you in the midst of expanding interests. There are planetary trends around that show you giving at least some time to the needs of family members but you will still not be over-keen to give yourself to Christmas absolutely. By the evening you could be possessed by a warm glow and permit a little more sentimentality.

25 MONDAY
Moon Age Day 7   Moon Sign Pisces

Energy levels will be extremely high on Christmas Day and you can expect to be the life and soul of the party. There is time to fit in almost everything you would wish and there will be surprises in store that are amazing, even by the standards of this particular day. There is a tremendous sense of warmth about right now.

26 TUESDAY
Moon Age Day 8   Moon Sign Pisces

This is a day during which you need to vent some of your pent-up frustrations. These can probably be dispersed simply by getting a change of scenery and by enjoying something different from the Christmas norm. If the weather is good you might opt for a walk in the country or by the coast. Whatever you choose, variety is essential.

27 WEDNESDAY
Moon Age Day 9   Moon Sign Aries

A high social profile remains your forte and there is no real sign of anything slowing down for today at least. There are some fascinating people around – the sort of individuals that inspire change and excitement without really trying. That's a bandwagon you can happily jump aboard and interesting times abound.

28 THURSDAY
Moon Age Day 10   Moon Sign Aries

If you happen to be working today it is a fact that new opportunities for advancement could easily present themselves. Most Leos will still be in the midst of the festivities and if your time is your own, give some hours to thoughts about the future. Now is as good a time for planning as you are likely to encounter this month.

29 FRIDAY
Moon Age Day 11   Moon Sign Taurus

Now you benefit most from having something new and interesting to do, so maybe it's time to take a good look again at some of those presents you received. You are very focused, even if there isn't too much you can approach in a practical sense. Just a tinge of restlessness and impatience is beginning to show itself at some stage today.

30 SATURDAY   *Moon Age Day 12   Moon Sign Taurus*

This is the perfect time to be assertive and to make it plain how you feel about specific issues. You tend to achieve your objectives fairly easily and without upsetting anyone on the way. Family members will be demanding your attention constantly but bearing in mind the time of year that probably isn't very surprising.

31 SUNDAY   *Moon Age Day 13   Moon Sign Gemini*

The last day of year means business as usual for many Leos. You may have positive dealings with a business partner and you have a great talent for commanding respect from almost anyone. You remain, to the last moment of the year, a born organiser, sure of yourself and happy to take on anything that looks lucrative.

LEO:
2018 DIARY PAGES

LEO:
YOUR YEAR IN BRIEF

Expect some startling events to proceed at a fast pace at the start of the year. During January, and especially in February, prepare for one or two surprises, though most of these should be positive in nature. You should be throwing yourself into things at the start of the year and it appears that, as a consequence, material gains are likely to be significant, even if you don't notice them until later.

March and April could be somewhat less eventful. This is probably no bad thing because you began the year with such gusto that it was always going to be difficult to keep up the pace. Thoughtful and now more willing to listen to what others are telling you, your actions in April especially could lead to very interesting events, and perhaps advancement, especially at work. Emotionally speaking, not everyone is as settled as you are, so try to help.

With May and June comes a need to relax but because you are always so busy this is hard to achieve. Routines can be something of a drag at this time, so take care not to get bogged down in situations. Keep a sense of proportion when it comes to affairs of the heart but be just as bold as you need to be when it comes to telling someone very special how you feel about them.

With the arrival of the high summer you are likely to be at your most potent and will be firing on all cylinders. With new starts and new opportunities popping up all the time during July and August there is little doubt that you are fully on form and simply charging towards your chosen destinations. Don't spend too long looking at the faults and failings of others or you may come face to face with some of your own.

The year advances at a startling rate and there could be a few decisions that need to be made. In at least some cases, it's likely that you won't want to make them. September and October are the months when you need to be decisive and to let yourself and others know that you mean business. In a financial and a romantic sense this can be a good interlude and one that, once again, brings a number of surprises.

The final two months of the year, November and December, may see a slackening of the pace at first, followed by a great rush to the finishing line of the year end. Start new projects of any kind in November and before you know it you will be winning races. Christmas may be especially memorable this year and could bring some special surprises and some fairly startling new encounters.

January
2018

1 MONDAY
Moon Age Day 14   Moon Sign Gemini

Make this the most adventurous start to the year that you can manage. Others might be resting but your resolve is strong and your capacity for going it alone has seldom been better that it is at present. Constructive criticism may be necessary in the case of partnerships, but be tactful or this might not go down too well.

2 TUESDAY
Moon Age Day 15   Moon Sign Cancer

Today is very good with regard to your social life, in fact much better than has been the case for quite a while. You are still on a steep learning curve and you may have to start again at the beginning with regard to a project that has not turned out as you would have wished. Be patient and accept that things really will come good in the end.

3 WEDNESDAY
Moon Age Day 16   Moon Sign Cancer

It may be that doubt and uncertainty will dog your footsteps today. You always want to know where you are going and you can get quite frustrated when the road ahead is not clear. When it comes to impressing other people it looks as though you are being much more successful than you realise so trust your instincts.

4 THURSDAY
Moon Age Day 17   Moon Sign Leo

Most of what you take on today should turn out very well for you. The monthly lunar high means you should avoid any frustration and enjoy a better strike rate than you have managed for a week or two. Don't be too quick to take offence because you can be sure that people are genuinely on your side. Your creative potential has rarely been better than it is now

5 FRIDAY
Moon Age Day 18   Moon Sign Leo

Your competitive spirit is on show under present trends. It is true that you are not always the most patient of people but just at the moment, be content to hold your horses. In doing so, you will help yourself immeasurably, and also help others do what is important to them.

6 SATURDAY
Moon Age Day 19   Moon Sign Virgo

Present planetary positions indicate great determination and the sort of will that typifies your zodiac sign. Give it all you've got at work and be bold enough to speak your mind on all occasions. With a combination of certainty and intuition you are sure to go far – in fact just as far as you can imagine.

7 SUNDAY
Moon Age Day 20   Moon Sign Virgo

All intellectual pursuits are well favoured today. Show the world just how clever you are and make yourself indispensable on the way. Slowly but surely you are get where you need to be even if at times this does not seem to be the case. Attitude is all-important when you are dealing with any aspect of love.

8 MONDAY
Moon Age Day 21   Moon Sign Libra

Your domestic life should be running fairly smoothly at the moment, even if you are having to work overtime in order to keep people following your chosen path. In practical matters, remain as patient as your Leo nature allows you to be and avoid giving the impression that you know everything.

9 TUESDAY
Moon Age Day 22   Moon Sign Libra

The pursuit of pleasure is likely to bring you the greatest happiness today and you will be at your very best when you are socialising and having a good time. It might take a while to achieve some of your objectives but life is not a race and there should be plenty of time for you to take it slowly and steadily.

10 WEDNESDAY   *Moon Age Day 23   Moon Sign Scorpio*

If there are any mundane or routine jobs to be done, now is the time to get them sorted out. Your patience is better than would normally be the case and there are planetary helpers around that keep you calm, cool and collected. This should be a day of possibilities and some very important projects are beginning now.

11 THURSDAY   *Moon Age Day 24   Moon Sign Scorpio*

Whatever you decide to do today, undertake it in a spirit of open-minded optimism. You will be quite amazed with what you get done and when it comes to popularity you can be sure that you are the top of the tree. It appears that everyone wants to know your name and will relying on your good advice.

12 FRIDAY   *Moon Age Day 25   Moon Sign Scorpio*

Focus most of your attention on intellectual matters today and think situations through carefully before you make any hard and fast decisions. New personalities could be entering your life, with the possibility of long-term friendships developing. Even though it is winter you really should be spending some of your time out of doors.

13 SATURDAY   *Moon Age Day 26   Moon Sign Sagittarius*

When it comes to your friendships you are likely to be looking for some peace and quiet this weekend. You won't feel like getting involved in any disputes, and this a good thing too because there are better ways to sort things out. Look for people from the past coming along who could just have some answers for you that are relevant to the long-term future.

14 SUNDAY   *Moon Age Day 27   Moon Sign Sagittarius*

Generally speaking you are now inclined to see the good in those around you. This makes you a good friend and also ensures you of increasing popularity. Get away from situations and people who have a tendency to hold you back and wherever possible go for gold, especially in sporting activities.

15 MONDAY *Moon Age Day 28*   *Moon Sign Capricorn*

Avoid playing the martyr today. It doesn't suit you and you aren't that good at doing it in any case. If things happen that you think are unfair you need to speak out, though gently of course. On a personal footing you seem to be getting it just right and the truly romantic side of the Leo nature is clearly on display under present planetary trends.

16 TUESDAY *Moon Age Day 0*   *Moon Sign Capricorn*

During this time a new friendship may be starting and it looks as though you will be quite keen to make the most of what those around you have to offer. Leo is now less selfish than can occasionally be the case and you will quite happily put yourself out to offer some timely assistance to people who really need it.

17 WEDNESDAY *Moon Age Day 1*   *Moon Sign Capricorn*

In a philosophical mood, you will be quite happy to sit and scratch your head for a while instead of pitching in and getting yourself in a muddle. Working out how and why things work in the way they do should prove to be quite entertaining and is a good way to pass some time now.

18 THURSDAY *Moon Age Day 2*   *Moon Sign Aquarius*

Today is not a good time to take any sort of risk. This is the time of the lunar low when your abilities may not be all that you would wish. Be as determined as you need to be but also learn that there are moments for activity but other times when it would be far better to wait and see. Someone you haven't seen for ages could return to your life.

19 FRIDAY *Moon Age Day 3*   *Moon Sign Aquarius*

Rein things in a little and be willing to take your path through life more steadily. The results of doing so could really surprise you and bring benefits that you never expected. By this evening you should be quite prepared to let matters run their course. Take particular care with personal attachments.

20 SATURDAY
Moon Age Day 4   Moon Sign Pisces

Whilst you are presently keen to satisfy your own needs and wants in life, it looks as though people close to you will be expecting a great deal from you. It won't always be easy to satisfy everyone's demands and there might be occasions today when it would be much better to simply admit that you don't have all the answers.

21 SUNDAY
Moon Age Day 5   Moon Sign Pisces

Make the most of whatever is happening on the social front. It is likely that you could be appealing in the eyes of people who are definitely in a position to help you, so don't be afraid to call on the positive resources of colleagues and friends alike. After all, they are only returning favours.

22 MONDAY
Moon Age Day 6   Moon Sign Pisces

Use your energy to plan some moves at work and to help others to get ahead in their chosen career. You would now be particularly good at offering advice to younger people or to those who are making a genuine fresh start in life. Leo often champions the underdog and that is exactly what you tend to do at this time.

23 TUESDAY
Moon Age Day 7   Moon Sign Aries

One-to-one relationships may seem to have a few drawbacks at the moment, thanks to the present position of Venus in your solar chart. You can be too thoughtful for your own good and inclined to see personal problems where none really exist. It won't be long before times change and you are back to your normal self.

24 WEDNESDAY
Moon Age Day 8   Moon Sign Aries

Travel both local and distant should prove to be interesting and you won't get everything you really want from life at the moment if you choose to stay in the same place all the time. Whether or not you can persuade other people to make trips with you is another matter; a few stick-in-the mud types may surround you now.

25 THURSDAY — *Moon Age Day 9   Moon Sign Taurus*

There is something of a search for inner security going on within you at this time and you are a little more vulnerable to supposed emotional attacks than would normally be the case. In reality you are probably making mountains out of molehills. Get on with something practical and leave the psychology to others for the moment.

26 FRIDAY — *Moon Age Day 10   Moon Sign Taurus*

Your self-confidence is definitely increasing and as the month advances you are getting ever better ideas about the way you want things to be in your life. Not everyone is quite as progressive as you are, which is why it sometimes feels as though you are towing people along behind you. Leo is now on top form but take life steadily.

27 SATURDAY — *Moon Age Day 11   Moon Sign Gemini*

Don't begin anything new until you have finished a present project. Leo can usually deal with half a dozen different jobs at the same time but for the moment you need to be quite discriminating. A great triumph stands before you but it may need every ounce of your concentration to get things right.

28 SUNDAY — *Moon Age Day 12   Moon Sign Gemini*

The needs and wants of those close to you may be of great concern to you right now and it looks as though you are going to be especially sympathetic, both today and for several more days to come. There is a lot taking place in your solar chart at this time which makes you think more deeply. Your actions are now well considered.

29 MONDAY — *Moon Age Day 13   Moon Sign Cancer*

New meetings are likely to be the order of the day this week. Don't lock yourself away at home, no matter what the weather is doing. It would be better by far to get out and about as much as you can. Friends might have some novel ideas for how to spend this evening and joining them could be fun.

30 TUESDAY   *Moon Age Day 14   Moon Sign Cancer*

You know what you want and as is usually the case for you, you also have a very good idea about how to get it. Don't be too keen to put yourself forward for jobs you don't really understand. It would be far better at the moment to do a little homework. That way you will be able to show just how efficient and competent you are.

31 WEDNESDAY   *Moon Age Day 15   Moon Sign Leo*

You should be creating situations that can turn out to be fun for everyone concerned. This is the most attractive side of Leo because your imagination is strong and you can see through others as if they were made of glass. Look out for more vulnerable people today, as well as animals that may need your protection more than usual.

February
2018

1 THURSDAY
Moon Age Day 16   Moon Sign Leo

Optimism should be in plentiful supply and it looks as though you are going to get a good deal of what you want today. It might take you a while to get used to something new but you are a quick learner and you can afford to take on appealing challenges all the time. You have good judgement at your disposal now that the lunar high is around.

2 FRIDAY
Moon Age Day 17   Moon Sign Virgo

Fulfilment may not be found in relationships today unless you put in that bit of effort that can make all the difference. Your mind is working quickly and you instinctively know how to bring others round to your point of view. Responding to a social invitation could be the best thing you do before the weekend.

3 SATURDAY
Moon Age Day 18   Moon Sign Virgo

You could have a sudden intuitive idea that is both inspirational and potentially successful. Don't dismiss such thoughts from your mind, no matter how quirky they may at first appear to be. When it comes to work you can think about it wherever you happen to be and social networking is one good way to promote your own interests during this weekend.

4 SUNDAY
Moon Age Day 19   Moon Sign Libra

Group matters are now favourably highlighted and you will be able to bring others round to your way of thinking. If you are the head of a team, either in your work or socially, now is the time to make certain everyone knows what you want. Explain yourself carefully and be prepared to do so again if necessary.

5 MONDAY
Moon Age Day 20   Moon Sign Libra

A lift comes from the direction of friends and it is towards them that you are likely to turn time and again across the next couple of days. You are now taking life much more in your stride than you might have done for a few weeks. Because of this you are also very relaxed and this shows in the way you treat everyone you encounter today.

6 TUESDAY
Moon Age Day 21   Moon Sign Libra

Prospects look very good in a practical sense, especially if you are at work today. Any small headaches you have been experiencing recently are likely to be blown away on a breeze of optimism, which is always a good sign for you. The attitude of a friend might surprise you and it's likely they really need your support.

7 WEDNESDAY
Moon Age Day 22   Moon Sign Scorpio

Confusion could be the keyword today unless you take stock regularly and make sure that you finish one job before you get started with another. Avoid arguments at home and also in your working life and let others have their own way if it is so very important to them. Standing alone on very important issues is worthy but risky at present.

8 THURSDAY
Moon Age Day 23   Moon Sign Scorpio

You may enjoy taking on new challenges but make sure you are not starting off up mountains you can't hope to climb. Some caution is still indicated, together with a degree of common sense which is usually second nature to you. For now you are not thinking quite as clearly as you generally would and that might mean seeking advice.

9 FRIDAY
Moon Age Day 24   Moon Sign Sagittarius

You could so easily be drawn into something you don't want to do but it is possible that once you get started you will be charmed by what happens. Be open-minded and consider some ideas you haven't entertained before. It seems as though you will be doing all you can to build social contacts today.

10 SATURDAY   *Moon Age Day 25   Moon Sign Sagittarius*

Be on the lookout for all the many opportunities that are likely to be coming your way at any time now. It's well into February and there may just be a hint of spring in the air. If you can't sense it, then find some way to make it so. A bright and happy disposition is as good a way as any to get going. How attractive you look to others at this time.

11 SUNDAY   *Moon Age Day 26   Moon Sign Sagittarius*

Mental discipline is hard to achieve and there are times today when you could feel somewhat confused and inclined to do the wrong thing. This could be especially true in personal attachments. Be a little careful not to over-indulge around now and if anything you should tend to abstain from too much good living, at least for a day or two.

12 MONDAY   *Moon Age Day 27   Moon Sign Capricorn*

Benefits now come through partnerships, both personal and practical. Avoid doing all the running yourself and rely on others at times. Relax when you can, especially this evening, and get on side with a loved one who may think you have been ignoring them. It's amazing what a few kind words can do.

13 TUESDAY   *Moon Age Day 28   Moon Sign Capricorn*

You probably feel in need of the bright lights in a social sense. At the same time you could be suffering from too much darkness and winter weather. Leos who are heading off for a little winter sun around now are the luckiest of all, but even if this is not the case you should try to avoid staying in gloomy places. Turn on the power.

14 WEDNESDAY   *Moon Age Day 29   Moon Sign Aquarius*

Take your time and be patient Leo, otherwise you could find yourself getting into a muddle about something that generally wouldn't bother you at all. It's possible you are trying to rush your fences too much – something that is inclined to happen whilst the lunar low is around. Stand back and take stock and don't act rashly, at least not for now.

15 THURSDAY
Moon Age Day 0   Moon Sign Aquarius

Today you need to be as sensitive and intuitive as you can possibly make yourself. The more you bear in mind the thoughts and wishes of those around you, the easier your path will become later. Allow time to pass without thinking that you should be doing something in every minute. Put your feet up and let others take the strain.

16 FRIDAY
Moon Age Day 1   Moon Sign Aquarius

You are good at manipulating events right now, using a combination of common sense and your magnetic personality. However, you can't control everything and there may be times right now when you will have to rely on the good offices of friends or colleagues. Don't be frightened to ask if you need a favour.

17 SATURDAY
Moon Age Day 2   Moon Sign Pisces

This is a time to be cautious and to study the details of any business deal very carefully. If you have to sign a document, make sure you look at the small print first and don't be conned into thinking that the grass really is all that green on the other side of the fence. Sometimes you are best at sticking to what you know.

18 SUNDAY
Moon Age Day 3   Moon Sign Pisces

You should now feel happy and relaxed when you are with your friends. This is a good time to expand your social life and to show the world just how outgoing and cheerful you are. There should also be a chance to prove to someone that you are not quite as intense as they might have thought was the case.

19 MONDAY
Moon Age Day 4   Moon Sign Aries

Social functions should run harmoniously and even the people who usually get on your nerves are less likely to do so while you are in your present frame of mind. Anyone who wants something from you is more likely to ask because you are so very approachable. This could be the happiest part of February in many ways.

20 TUESDAY
Moon Age Day 5   Moon Sign Aries

Be just a little careful today, otherwise you could become involved in conflicts that are quite unnecessary. This may not be your own fault because certain individuals are not behaving in a strictly rational way. The best way forward is to get to the bottom of situations and find out what is really going on, even if you have to do some digging.

21 WEDNESDAY
Moon Age Day 6   Moon Sign Taurus

In between necessary bouts of activity you work at your best when you can retreat slightly into a different sort of reality. This is not really like Leo and a few people might wonder if there is something wrong with you. Let them know that you are quite happy but that you are not really in the market for pushing yourself too hard just now.

22 THURSDAY
Moon Age Day 7   Moon Sign Taurus

Now your sensitivity increases and you show the caring and compassionate side of your nature. All of the attention you have been giving to family and friends is certainly not wasted and it proves to those around you that there is far more to Leo than the progressive, go-getting individual you can be.

23 FRIDAY
Moon Age Day 8   Moon Sign Taurus

There could be some tricky finances to deal with, especially regarding business, or perhaps a family inheritance or some other domestic issue. Try to be patient with people who don't fully understand the way things work and stay away from causing arguments that are not necessary and which won't solve anything at all.

24 SATURDAY
Moon Age Day 9   Moon Sign Gemini

Now there may be events that lead to feelings of escapism, which is actually quite unusual for Leo. As a result you could feel slightly ill at ease with yourself and nowhere near as confident as would normally be the case. If you don't know how to do something the best way forward is to ask someone who does.

25 SUNDAY   *Moon Age Day 10   Moon Sign Gemini*

You now feel more compassion and sympathy for others than has been the case even during this quite sensitive period. Working for and on behalf of those who don't have either your confidence or your natural ability will seem quite attractive and you can get a great deal out of providing a platform for the less capable to work from.

26 MONDAY   *Moon Age Day 11   Moon Sign Cancer*

This should be a very beneficial time as far as group activities are concerned. You quite naturally become the leader in many situations and this is certainly likely to be the case at this time. Present planetary positions make you especially good at getting your personal affairs well in order.

27 TUESDAY   *Moon Age Day 12   Moon Sign Cancer*

There are new and promising possibilities at work at this stage of the working week. Today would be a good time to get something you want from someone who is higher up the career ladder than you are. You have the confidence to do the right thing when in romantic situations and there is no doubting your present charm.

28 WEDNESDAY   *Moon Age Day 13   Moon Sign Leo*

This ought to be a good day in an all-round sense. Play the percentage cards and you are likely to come up trumps. There are gains to be made in terms of love and for some Leos at this time there is also the chance of a brand new relationship beginning. Don't waste time because you can turn things around easily.

March

2018

1 THURSDAY
Moon Age Day 14   Moon Sign Leo

Today is definitely the right time to set new plans into action. Don't delay and use the power of the lunar high to your best advantage. You should be extra good with money around now and well able to see ahead of yourself when it comes to taking practical and financial decisions. Most of all you will feel like having a good time.

2 FRIDAY
Moon Age Day 15   Moon Sign Virgo

You could feel as though people are out to get you today but in fact you are probably feeling slightly persecuted for no good reason. Part of this is because everything went your way across the last couple of days and you won't take kindly to the odd reversal. Don't let false worries get the better of you.

3 SATURDAY
Moon Age Day 16   Moon Sign Virgo

Your popularity is likely to increase significantly during this part of the weekend. What's more your relationship with the world at large has probably never been better than it is right now. Use this positive period to build up your influence and to gain the help and support of people who are in a good position to do you a favour.

4 SUNDAY
Moon Age Day 17   Moon Sign Libra

In a mental sense you are clearly very sharp today and you could pit your wits against just about anyone. What is probably more important is that you will also be very funny. Everyone will be happy to have you around and will be giving back to you at least some of the goodwill you are showing to just about everyone you encounter.

5 MONDAY   *Moon Age Day 18   Moon Sign Libra*

Intellectually you continue to be sharp today and you are in a good position to further your own interests in a number of different directions. Getting to grips with what may have seemed like a sticky problem only a few days ago should now be very much easier and you will be able to show just what a good organiser you can be.

6 TUESDAY   *Moon Age Day 19   Moon Sign Scorpio*

The emotional side of life is likely to dominate today and you probably should not expect too much in the way of constructive help from those around you. In reality the problem lies in your own mind but with present planetary trends it could be hard to see this. What you can do is keep yourself and others laughing as much as possible.

7 WEDNESDAY   *Moon Age Day 20   Moon Sign Scorpio*

A new optimism is starting to enter your life and slowly but surely you feel as though you are making the sort of progress that probably was not easy to achieve across the last couple of weeks at least. You are confident that you are in the right, even if on occasions you have to register the fact that others do not agree with you.

8 THURSDAY   *Moon Age Day 21   Moon Sign Sagittarius*

Today should mark an optimistic, self-confident time. You should have improved vitality and a feeling that you could climb a mountain if necessary, and without significant effort. One thing you won't care for is being told what you should do, especially by people for whom you already have little or no respect.

9 FRIDAY   *Moon Age Day 22   Moon Sign Sagittarius*

Group relationships should be settled and happy, if only because, once again, people are turning to you to make most of the decisions. Being in the driving seat is definitely the place you prefer to be and there are some significant gains to be made in your financial state. Don't gamble too much but take opportunities that arise naturally.

10 SATURDAY   *Moon Age Day 23   Moon Sign Sagittarius*

Now there is likely to be a peak of sorts and this shows itself most for Leos who work at the weekend. It is in this sphere of your life that you can make the greatest impression and you need to be right on the ball when it comes to proving your worth. Many Leo people treat life as a competition and at this time you are winning.

11 SUNDAY   *Moon Age Day 24   Moon Sign Capricorn*

It is possible that you will experience disharmony in your associations with certain other people. This won't be everyone but there are the dominant types around with whom you often cross swords. This is partly because you prefer to be in charge yourself and don't take too kindly to anyone else trying to rule your roost.

12 MONDAY   *Moon Age Day 25   Moon Sign Capricorn*

Excellent trends surround your life and in particular social activities that are taking place at this time. Group ventures look good and many people should look to you to make the running. Being in charge of things is rarely a problem for you and you revel in the fact that so much trust is coming your way.

13 TUESDAY   *Moon Age Day 26   Moon Sign Aquarius*

Stand by for the arrival of the lunar low which, if you are not prepared for it, could take the wind out of your sails at a moment's notice. If things do seem to be going wrong, try to realise that this is just a short phase. In no time at all, new and strong influences from other planetary directions will take command of your life.

14 WEDNESDAY   *Moon Age Day 27   Moon Sign Aquarius*

Although your judgement may not be perfect today and you could feel as though you are not firing on all cylinders, you can still get ahead by the sheer dogged determination that is so much a part of your nature. You seem to have many things arranged quite well and in advance. These facts will make the lunar low pass more quickly and successfully.

15 THURSDAY   *Moon Age Day 28   Moon Sign Aquarius*

You may now start to receive a degree of recognition for things you did in the past. Some of this is likely to be associated with your social life but there are also practical issues that see you winning through. At the same time you could be slightly stubborn and you certainly won't knuckle under if you feel you are correct.

16 FRIDAY   *Moon Age Day 29   Moon Sign Pisces*

Friends are likely to be very supportive and their mere presence in your life could stimulate some interesting ideas that you will want to put into practice later. This is also a good time for the romantically inclined Leo. You are able to show your sensitive side and to think up the most endearing words of love.

17 SATURDAY   *Moon Age Day 0   Moon Sign Pisces*

Now you are prone to being led up the garden path by someone. As a rule Leo is the most astute of all the zodiac signs but just at present you are not fully aware when it comes to your natural intuition. Don't sign documents today or at least if you must make sure you have read them fully.

18 SUNDAY   *Moon Age Day 1   Moon Sign Aries*

If you are unsure about your goals and objectives at the moment, this would be a good time to stop and take stock. Things will become much more hectic in the days ahead, while at the moment there is time for reflection. Get plenty of rest and try to avoid taking on jobs that are not your responsibility.

19 MONDAY   *Moon Age Day 2   Moon Sign Aries*

You may desire freedom but this is a commodity that isn't all that easy to find in the midst of many responsibilities. There ought to be at least part of the day you can call your own and you will probably choose to find a little quiet corner for yourself. This slower period will soon be over but for now just chill.

20 TUESDAY   *Moon Age Day 3   Moon Sign Aries*

Intuition can be a powerful tool, especially so at the present time. It would take someone extremely clever to fool you in any way and you show yourself to be astute for others, as well as for yourself. Don't take no for an answer regarding an issue that has been uppermost in your mind but do try to compromise.

21 WEDNESDAY   *Moon Age Day 4   Moon Sign Taurus*

Where your love life is concerned you may need to be paying significant attention to what others are saying. This can be difficult because although it is important to monitor the way your partner is feeling, this is not a time during which you should listen to gossip. Turn on that intuition and back your own hunches.

22 THURSDAY   *Moon Age Day 5   Moon Sign Taurus*

Now you are able to deal positively with a past issue and your ability to look ahead becomes better than has been the case for some weeks. Attitude is especially important in your working life and it is likely that you will be asked to take on some task that looks difficult. Don't worry – it's something you will cope with easily.

23 FRIDAY   ☿   *Moon Age Day 6   Moon Sign Gemini*

You have a good ability to get down below the surface of situations and to see the motivations at their centre. Once again it is very important to use your intuition and to make decisions according to instinct. It seems as though the world is now definitely on your side for most of the time and new possibilities come from all around you.

24 SATURDAY   ☿   *Moon Age Day 7   Moon Sign Gemini*

Avoid routines at all costs because they are almost certain to get on your nerves at this time. It would be far better to take on a dozen different tasks today than to allow yourself to become bored. Leo is really working well now and you bring joy to your own life and to that of others, simply by being yourself.

25 SUNDAY ☿ *Moon Age Day 8   Moon Sign Cancer*

A relationship issue could give you pause for thought but is unlikely to be allowed to get in the way of what is a very progressive period. If anything you may be expecting just a little too much from yourself and could afford to take a few hours to think matters through. Take a trip with your partner, family members or friends.

26 MONDAY ☿ *Moon Age Day 9   Moon Sign Cancer*

Dominating and coercive attitudes are to be avoided, particularly in your home environment. What might not help situations at all is the fact that those around you are feeling competitive and argumentative too. Stick to friends and colleagues if you can today because in their company you are far less likely to go off the deep end.

27 TUESDAY ☿ *Moon Age Day 10   Moon Sign Leo*

The lunar high is known for fortunate circumstances and you are well able to get what you want from life while it is around. Don't sit there waiting for life to hand you something, rather go out and make it work on your behalf. There are likely to be especially pronounced gains to be made at work and in fact anywhere where positive action counts.

28 WEDNESDAY ☿ *Moon Age Day 11   Moon Sign Leo*

You can exercise leadership quite well under almost any circumstances but much more so when the lunar high comes to visit you. With the Moon in your zodiac sign of Leo you are confident and striking to see. Don't be at all surprised if there are a few admirers around during this stage of the week and accept what they have to offer.

29 THURSDAY ☿ *Moon Age Day 12   Moon Sign Virgo*

This particular Thursday finds you highly motivated, unusual in your thought processes and attitudes and simply dying to get on with things. Not everyone around you has the same idea but when it matters the most you can get your own way. Home-based matters should be easier today and romance is likely to shine out noticeably.

30 FRIDAY ☿ *Moon Age Day 13 Moon Sign Virgo*

You are certainly innovative when it comes to leadership issues but at the same time you take a low-key attitude to most aspects of life. Don't be too willing to put yourself out for someone who has proved to be unreliable in the past and listen carefully to your inner voice when it comes to taking financial risks. They may be a bridge too far.

31 SATURDAY ☿ *Moon Age Day 14 Moon Sign Libra*

You are now at your most creative but you shouldn't allow your imagination to run away with you. A positive attitude is fine and so is a fertile mind but be realistic and in the main stick to what you know. Finances are likely to be fairly strong and you could afford to take the odd small chance that you wouldn't have considered before.

April

2018

1 SUNDAY
☿ *Moon Age Day 15   Moon Sign Libra*

Wide awake and alert today, it is quite unlikely that anyone will get ahead of you. On the contrary you can see a scam ten miles away and should act accordingly. Give yourself a pat on the back for a job well done but don't leave it at that. Push your way through to an even better victory than you expected.

2 MONDAY
☿ *Moon Age Day 16   Moon Sign Scorpio*

You will now be especially sensitive to the way other people are feeling, which will be useful when it comes to assisting friends who have got themselves into something of a jam. Whilst they might find it difficult to see their path ahead, you will be able to sort things out in a minute. You ally sound common sense with practical application.

3 TUESDAY
☿ *Moon Age Day 17   Moon Sign Scorpio*

Communications with others are likely to go smoothly enough and you can show what you are made of when it comes to talking yourself both in and out of certain situations. Love looks good and romantic bells should be ringing in your heart. It also seems you may have new admirers.

4 WEDNESDAY
☿ *Moon Age Day 18   Moon Sign Scorpio*

Though professional matters might contain a few challenges, you are likely to rise to these almost immediately and you are well able to show colleagues and your boss exactly what sort of stuff you are made of. You are also quite intuitive around now and can foretell the outcome of many situations without too much difficulty.

5 THURSDAY   ☿ *Moon Age Day 19*   *Moon Sign Sagittarius*

Emotional responses could now cloud your judgement and it would be wise to avoid them at all costs. Use your practical common sense and not your heart when it comes to assessing both people and situations. In a verbal sense this is definitely no time to shoot from the hip and things work out much better if you think before you speak.

6 FRIDAY   ☿ *Moon Age Day 20*   *Moon Sign Sagittarius*

You are mentally alert today and so won't fall for anyone's charms when you know instinctively that they are trying to dupe you in some way. You should also be looking out for friends and loved ones, some of whom are not quite as worldly-wise as you are. Give some thought to a newer and better way of getting away from old routines.

7 SATURDAY   ☿ *Moon Age Day 21*   *Moon Sign Capricorn*

If you want the finer things in life, this is the time to go out and get them. This might involve spending a little money but that's fine, just as long as you are getting good value. You can achieve a great deal now if you are diplomatic, especially with people who have it in their power to do you a great deal of personal good.

8 SUNDAY   ☿ *Moon Age Day 22*   *Moon Sign Capricorn*

What a great time this is for socialising. It doesn't matter whether you know the people concerned or not as you are as good with strangers at the moment as you are with your best friends. People want to have you around and will make it plain that they value your opinions and even your jokes.

9 MONDAY   ☿ *Moon Age Day 23*   *Moon Sign Capricorn*

Pay attention and make sure that you know what is going on around you and you should gain some wisdom in return. You can also learn from experience, which is the best possible teacher of all to a Leo. Make arrangements well in advance and don't change your plans at the last minute just to please someone else.

10 TUESDAY ☿ *Moon Age Day 24 Moon Sign Aquarius*

This is a time when others might tend to impose on you. The lunar low is here and the Moon occupies your opposite zodiac sign of Aquarius. Not everyone seems to be trustworthy, though it is entirely possible that you are getting certain situations completely out of proportion. Pace yourself and do first those jobs that are most necessary.

11 WEDNESDAY ☿ *Moon Age Day 25 Moon Sign Aquarius*

Today you could run out of steam very quickly and it would be best to let others do some of the hard work, whilst you sit back and supervise. This might not extend to your partner, who may feel instantly put upon if you ask them to do too much for you. However, a little charm can go a long way and if you really turn it on you can get anything.

12 THURSDAY ☿ *Moon Age Day 26 Moon Sign Pisces*

You are now advised to put your versatility to good use. As a result you come to a better understanding of the direction in which your life is travelling and you can make the very most of any opportunity that presents itself. It may take longer than you wish to get certain things done but this is only because you are rather impatient now.

13 FRIDAY ☿ *Moon Age Day 27 Moon Sign Pisces*

You need to guard against carelessness today because there is every chance you could get yourself into some sort of scrape that will be difficult to sort out. All the same, if you maintain your sense of humour there is not likely to be anything taking place you will find impossible to deal with. You should be really charming company in a social sense.

14 SATURDAY ☿ *Moon Age Day 28 Moon Sign Pisces*

When it comes to putting yourself in the spotlight there is no doubt that you are now at your best. People will automatically turn to you for assistance and you should find the way ahead quite easy to negotiate. Self-confident and assertive, your progress should not let up.

15 SUNDAY
Moon Age Day 29   Moon Sign Aries

Income and resources are highlighted today so this is a time to get your financial house in order. If you think about situations carefully you should be able to have the penny and the bun but only if you turn your personal radar up to full. A recent purchase could turn out to have been a wise investment.

16 MONDAY
Moon Age Day 0   Moon Sign Aries

This is a very favourable time to unearth new information and to get what you want from a whole host of situations. There is little to stand in your way because the planets are on your side and you should be filled with energy and enthusiasm. This should be the start of what could turn out to be a very good week indeed.

17 TUESDAY
Moon Age Day 1   Moon Sign Taurus

At work you are efficient and can get things done in a fraction of the time colleagues can. This is going to get you noticed – usually for the right reasons but occasionally because of the wrong ones. You don't want to rub anyone up the wrong way so when you have done what you need to do, find ways to help others.

18 WEDNESDAY
Moon Age Day 2   Moon Sign Taurus

You could feel as though you have slightly over-extended yourself. This is not unusual for Leo when things are going well and it might be necessary to slow life down a little, so that you can catch up with yourself. The weekend is not all that far away and you should be planning something that is both exciting and ultimately profitable.

19 THURSDAY
Moon Age Day 3   Moon Sign Gemini

This would be a great time to find uses for old or ignored articles you thought you might never need again. The same is true with ideas you put on hold before because they may suddenly become relevant again. There is room for everyone in your life now, and you look out for family members and friends.

20 FRIDAY
Moon Age Day 4   Moon Sign Gemini

A change to a current plan might turn out to be a good thing and since you are the master of thinking on your feet you should be in a good position to pick up on unexpected opportunities. Get onside with people you know are going to be successful and they will give you a tow towards your own objectives.

21 SATURDAY
Moon Age Day 5   Moon Sign Cancer

A more optimistic time comes along and you have certainly come a long way since the beginning of this year. Don't bother yourself with pointless routines and be willing to dump certain things that are no longer of any use to you. When it comes to romance you are in the best position to make a good impression.

22 SUNDAY
Moon Age Day 6   Moon Sign Cancer

You possess plenty of physical energy and will be using this in all sorts of different ways. Confident in your own ability, and you may also be at the leading edge of a new idea that will fund your efforts for some weeks or months to come. Plan now for travel you are going to undertake later in the year.

23 MONDAY
Moon Age Day 7   Moon Sign Leo

Now you are likely to be at your most optimistic and you can visualise all the amazing possibilities that are surrounding you. Although you may feel more like having a good time than actually doing any solid work, there are bound to be ways in which you can mix business with pleasure. The lunar high makes you a winner in every sense.

24 TUESDAY
Moon Age Day 8   Moon Sign Leo

Most of your efforts will bear fruit whilst the Moon occupies your own zodiac sign and you can be fairly sure that luck will be on your side when it matters the most. In daily life you should be available to offer a helping hand when it is needed and you should also be willing to go that extra mile for someone who you have relied on in the past.

25 WEDNESDAY
Moon Age Day 9   Moon Sign Virgo

Other people are now more willing than ever to listen to your views and it is therefore worth taking time to explain yourself fully. Even people who have not been especially helpful in the past should now rally round to offer assistance and you are skilled at keeping everyone working together.

26 THURSDAY
Moon Age Day 10   Moon Sign Virgo

Getting your message across to others proves to be extremely important at the moment and you can be sure at least that they will be listening to what you have to say. Finding an attentive audience is certainly not difficult when you are so charismatic and good to know. Avoid arguments at all costs right now.

27 FRIDAY
Moon Age Day 11   Moon Sign Virgo

Social affairs and positive encounters with others continue to be of supreme importance to you at this time. How you come across to the world at large is very important because it sets the seal on the way those around you will be happy to help you out in the weeks ahead. Show off your charming side.

28 SATURDAY
Moon Age Day 12   Moon Sign Libra

Intellectual pursuits are favoured today and you have the chance to show everyone around you just how ingenious you are capable of being. By using a logical approach you might be able to dream up a better way of doing something that hasn't changed for years. This could be the start of a profitable period.

29 SUNDAY
Moon Age Day 13   Moon Sign Libra

There can be great changes coming along for you in a personal sense, though none of these are likely to work against your best interests. On the contrary, romantic attachments are strengthened and there ought to be a good chance for you to start a new relationship at any time now – if you have been looking for one, that is.

30 MONDAY   *Moon Age Day 14   Moon Sign Scorpio*

All financial matters and investments should be proceeding fairly smoothly at the moment and you should discover that there are new ways to make money that you didn't really think about before. Your present moves tend to be well planned and you will be associating with like-minded people.

May

2018

1 TUESDAY
Moon Age Day 15   Moon Sign Scorpio

There is now a powerful emphasis on personal security and you may be looking at many aspects of your life in order to work out how you can make yourself feel more comfortable. Gains can be made through co-operation and as a result of new friendships but there are also people around you may find difficult to trust too much.

2 WEDNESDAY
Moon Age Day 16   Moon Sign Sagittarius

You should be very much in harmony with others as the week progresses and you can get on side with people you didn't always like much in the past. Is it them who are now being more giving or you? That's a question only you can answer but it is a fact that you are starting to see certain situations from a totally different perspective.

3 THURSDAY
Moon Age Day 17   Moon Sign Sagittarius

It is possible that you need to curb your ego because you are now not quite as understanding of colleagues and even friends as you could be. Present planetary positions make you into a go-getter but it might be sensible to ask yourself whether some of what you are aiming for is either sensible or necessary.

4 FRIDAY
Moon Age Day 18   Moon Sign Sagittarius

It should be said that romance is close to you at this time and your love life is likely to be increasingly on your mind. If you have been without a personal attachment for a while, now would be as good a time as any to look around. In reality you may not have to do so because love could so easily come knocking on your door at some stage soon.

5 SATURDAY *Moon Age Day 19   Moon Sign Capricorn*

There could be a certain measure of luck in a financial sense and you will be quite happy to speculate a little in terms of time and money in order to further your objectives. Leo is famous for being willing to take a chance and although you would be wise not to put your entire salary on the next horse, it looks as though your hunches will pay off.

6 SUNDAY *Moon Age Day 20   Moon Sign Capricorn*

At this time you should find that money comes your way quite easily, even if it disappears out of another door just as quickly. You are definitely in an 'easy come, easy go' frame of mind, which is fine in some ways. Just be careful that you don't let something go that could be of tremendous use to you further down the road of life.

7 MONDAY *Moon Age Day 21   Moon Sign Aquarius*

Monday brings the return of the lunar low, so you should take care in some respects. You may not have your usual level of energy and there is a sense that some jobs would be best left to other people. Don't doubt your own mind today but leave far-reaching actions until the middle of the week.

8 TUESDAY *Moon Age Day 22   Moon Sign Aquarius*

Now is definitely not the best time to be locking horns with anyone in authority. Come to think of it this isn't a good period to fall out with anyone at all if you can avoid it. Steer your own careful path through the day and enjoy the small things of life. If you look around you it should be obvious that you have much that is worth your gratitude.

9 WEDNESDAY *Moon Age Day 23   Moon Sign Aquarius*

Pour constructive energy into work and also into your social and domestic life. There is little chance that you will run out of steam - or at least not easily. So, as the adage goes, strike while the iron is hot. Someone especially attractive is likely to be entering your life today or tomorrow so keep your eyes wide open.

10 THURSDAY *Moon Age Day 24   Moon Sign Pisces*

Something to do with finances could spoil your good mood. In all probability you will discover that a move you made some time ago has not worked out entirely as you would have wished. All the same, avoid a tendency to tamper with things too much and take a longer view if you can. Tonight would be a good time for words of love.

11 FRIDAY *Moon Age Day 25   Moon Sign Pisces*

Today your ideas are ingenious and are backed up by your instincts. There's no problem with your capacity to work hard and, all things considered, this could turn out to be one of the best days of the month. You are likely to be busy but remember not to skip meals and make sure that you keep regular habits.

12 SATURDAY *Moon Age Day 26   Moon Sign Aries*

Your quick thinking is likely to be of tremendous use to you between now and Monday. While other people are flapping about and wondering what to do, you put your best foot forward and make things happen. This trend is usually with you in some shape or form but is especially well catered for under present trends.

13 SUNDAY *Moon Age Day 27   Moon Sign Aries*

Saving is probably not your strength but you could do far worse than to put aside a little cash around now. If you have been saving madly in order to make a trip, you should now discover that you have achieved more than you thought. This is also a good time for travelling and for getting to see those people who have been missing from your life.

14 MONDAY *Moon Age Day 28   Moon Sign Taurus*

There is now a strong emphasis on personal security, which always turns up now and again in the life of a Leo. You want to be sure that everything is running the way it should and you will be looking closely at situations to ensure this is the case. Don't get too tied down by what others demand of you just now.

15 TUESDAY
Moon Age Day 0   Moon Sign Taurus

Look for intellectually stimulating company and for situations that make the sort of demands you enjoy. Don't sit in the background and wait for things to happen but get involved. When it comes to finances you could find that there is slightly more cash about than you expected to have at this stage of the month.

16 WEDNESDAY
Moon Age Day 1   Moon Sign Gemini

You should have a fairly bright and breezy attitude to life today and it is clear that you are more than willing to take things in your stride. This ought to be the start of a fairly good period for Leo when you are able to push forward with all sorts of plans, some of which have been kept in storage for quite some time.

17 THURSDAY
Moon Age Day 2   Moon Sign Gemini

It looks as though you now have a great deal of influence on your employer and on work situations generally and you should bear this in mind if you have been looking for a raise of salary or for some sort of advancement. People you haven't seen for ages could be making a new appearance in your life and bring new incentives.

18 FRIDAY
Moon Age Day 3   Moon Sign Cancer

Improved communications mean that you will have no trouble letting others know exactly how you feel about any kind of situation. This doesn't mean you will be in any way critical or grumpy in your approach. On the contrary, you seem to have what it takes to be charming to everyone and this has a bearing on the reactions you get.

19 SATURDAY
Moon Age Day 4   Moon Sign Cancer

Your imagination and sensitivity are stimulated by the present position of the Moon in your solar chart. There is just a slight chance that it will be necessary to withdraw from certain situations, especially if you feel as though too much is being expected of you. Stand by for a busier couple of days to come.

20 SUNDAY
Moon Age Day 5   Moon Sign Leo

The lunar high favours an up-front attitude and a determination to get things done. The more energy you put into one end of the equation of life, the greater are the results that appear at the other end. Don't spend any time today hanging around in the shadows. You need to be moving quickly towards each important and chosen objective.

21 MONDAY
Moon Age Day 6   Moon Sign Leo

Your optimism, self-confidence and sheer drive are very marked right now. It might not be possible to do everything you would wish in a professional sense but you do have what it takes to make waves. Good luck is going to be on your side and you possess that finesse of touch that can make all the difference in life.

22 TUESDAY
Moon Age Day 7   Moon Sign Leo

The lunar high is still around as today gets going but as the hours wear on you will find that you develop a greater desire for some sort of comfort. Whether this means you will be buying bars of chocolate or a new mattress remains to be seen but by the evening you may revel in the chance to just put your feet up.

23 WEDNESDAY
Moon Age Day 8   Moon Sign Virgo

Today sees a strong effort in the direction of building up your personal resources. You will probably have an hour or two to think about things and to make plans regarding your approach to finances in the weeks ahead. In some respects you will perhaps see this as a pivotal and very important period.

24 THURSDAY
Moon Age Day 9   Moon Sign Virgo

It seems as though there is so much happening around you that is interesting, it is difficult to know exactly what to get on with first. A plan of action may be necessary but that isn't remotely difficult for you. During today you might have to turn your attention to a family matter that you did not look at seriously enough before.

25 FRIDAY
Moon Age Day 10   Moon Sign Libra

There's no doubt about it, you are now thinking on your feet and making the sort of progress that would have seemed quite impossible a month or two ago. If it seems that there is still more you need to do, exercise a little patience and make certain today that you approach jobs one at a time, otherwise a muddle could ensue.

26 SATURDAY
Moon Age Day 11   Moon Sign Libra

Stay alongside friends this weekend and drop some of the responsibility for a day or two. You work very hard and so you sometimes feel the need to play hard too. In quieter moments you can look inside and see the sort of person living in there that doesn't always get out into the fresh air. Meditation is always necessary.

27 SUNDAY
Moon Age Day 12   Moon Sign Scorpio

Keep abreast of all current news because it is quite likely that something is happening out there in the wider world that has a strong bearing on your own life. This is a time to act with courage and confidence and to show your boss especially that you are up for a challenge and quite willing to go that extra yard if necessary.

28 MONDAY
Moon Age Day 13   Moon Sign Scorpio

Opt for some light relief if possible and refuse to take either yourself or anyone else too seriously. The more laughs you have today, the better things are likely to go for you. If there are any really intense people around you at this time, you have what it takes to bring them back to reality and to cause them to smile.

29 TUESDAY
Moon Age Day 14   Moon Sign Sagittarius

You always have very high goals, so much so that you expect a great deal of yourself. That's fine, just as long as you realise that you are human and that not everything will always work out exactly as you would wish. You may have to eat a slice of humble pie today and though you won't like it, it won't do you any harm.

30 WEDNESDAY   *Moon Age Day 15   Moon Sign Sagittarius*

You will find that you are now no longer willing to accept the status quo because the level of your ambition is going off the scale. You simply have to change things, whether others like it or not. Standard responses in conversations with certain people won't work today and you will discover that you need to be slightly ingenious.

31 THURSDAY   *Moon Age Day 16   Moon Sign Sagittarius*

You can expect the support of family members, especially the older generation. Leo always wants to prove things for itself but a degree of experience helps and you can sometimes avoid making a particular mistake by talking to someone who has been in a situation before. Be careful what you eat at present.

June

2018

1 FRIDAY
Moon Age Day 17   Moon Sign Capricorn

Creative pursuits are likely to go especially well and you seem to be acquiring skills you didn't have before. There is plenty to get your teeth into at the moment and finding time to do what takes your fancy might not be all that easy. Be on the lookout for new friendships and for ways to reconnect with past associations.

2 SATURDAY
Moon Age Day 18   Moon Sign Capricorn

Today you can be appealing to others on many different levels. With all the third house associations that are taking place in your solar chart now is the time to make a good impression on just about everyone. You should find it very easy to whisper words of love into the ear of someone special.

3 SUNDAY
Moon Age Day 19   Moon Sign Aquarius

Cool, calm and relaxed – that's what you need to be if you are going to enjoy, rather than endure, the lunar low this month. Pushing against situations will not work right now and you may as well get used to this right from the start. Be willing to watch and wait, and let those around you do the running.

4 MONDAY
Moon Age Day 20   Moon Sign Aquarius

Expect some self-doubt, delays and obstacles. None of these are serious and most of them are definitely temporary. Just do what you know is necessary but do not take any decisions with far-reaching implications and be as willing as possible to delegate. Moments spent alone could be important and helpful.

5 TUESDAY *Moon Age Day 21   Moon Sign Aquarius*

At work you are likely to be showing a great deal of initiative and plenty of drive. The rewards that can come your way around now could be significant, mainly as a result of the steady and consistent effort you have put in previously. There are gains to be made at work and a new form of co-operation beginning to develop.

6 WEDNESDAY *Moon Age Day 22   Moon Sign Pisces*

Outdoor pursuits, especially travel, are likely to be uppermost in your mind through the latter part of this week. You could also be quite sporting in your spare time and your naturally competitive nature is emphasised. If you make small mistakes at work don't worry because these are likely to be overlooked.

7 THURSDAY *Moon Age Day 23   Moon Sign Pisces*

You could show a marked tendency to get yourself involved in impulse buying, which can either work for you or against you. Just take care that you don't spend more than you can spare at the moment, especially since there could be some opportunities for travel coming up and some real bargains to be had if you keep your money intact for the moment.

8 FRIDAY *Moon Age Day 24   Moon Sign Aries*

You are in a good position to express your ideas, so don't hang around waiting but go out and find people to talk to. Today can be quite atmospheric in one way or another and the sheer force of your personality is really showing. Pay attention to casual conversations as they could turn out to be significant.

9 SATURDAY *Moon Age Day 25   Moon Sign Aries*

This is a time when you can readily start new projects and a phase of your life that works extremely well if you really push for what you want. Although most astrological trends are extremely good at the moment there could be just a slight feeling that something is about to go wrong. Avoid feeling pessimistic.

10 SUNDAY
Moon Age Day 26   Moon Sign Aries

Now you need to be quite careful to think before you speak. It is quite possible to give offence without remotely realising that this is what you are doing. If so, you will have to put in some extra effort later to make things right again. Better by far to moderate your tone before you begin to speak to people you recognise as being sensitive.

11 MONDAY
Moon Age Day 27   Moon Sign Taurus

Your ability to think carefully is definitely enhanced and although you may seem to be prevaricating as far as others are concerned, you know what you want and how to get it. For this reason alone, rely on your own intuition and don't be diverted off course by people who have their own agendas.

12 TUESDAY
Moon Age Day 28   Moon Sign Taurus

You can't keep a good Leo down and that fact is quite obvious at this stage of the month. It looks as though you will be very busy in a personal sense, and you should also be mixing freely with as many people as you can. There may be a slight tendency for you to burn the candle at both ends – but that's the Lion.

13 WEDNESDAY
Moon Age Day 0   Moon Sign Gemini

Communication with others now takes centre stage to a great extent. There are gains to be made in terms of personal achievements and you seem to impress the sort of people who were difficult to come to terms with before. Family members may expect a great deal of you and some care is necessary.

14 THURSDAY
Moon Age Day 1   Moon Sign Gemini

Don't be reluctant to ask favours from people who are in a more elevated position than the one you occupy right now. Aspiration is a very important factor in the lives of Leo people and you need to set your sights on something that hasn't been possible in the past but which now begins to look a great deal more likely.

15 FRIDAY
Moon Age Day 2   Moon Sign Cancer

Your domestic life should be pleasant and comfortable, adding to a greater sense of security at this time. With the weekend in view you could decide to up the pressure in terms of your social life. You are a born organiser and this really shows for the next few days. It's only to be hoped that others accept the role you are adopting.

16 SATURDAY
Moon Age Day 3   Moon Sign Cancer

This is a period during which things that are going on in the outside world should lift your spirits no end. Gains come from being in the right place at the right time and you are filled with enthusiasm to do something new. You should also wake up to an opportunity you seem to have completely missed before.

17 SUNDAY
Moon Age Day 4   Moon Sign Leo

The Moon is now back in your zodiac sign and that means the lunar high will be doing a great deal for your confidence. At the same time you are now involved in a very positive phase with regard to many areas of your life. The best adage to remember for now is to strike while the iron is hot!

18 MONDAY
Moon Age Day 5   Moon Sign Leo

Keep up the pressure to get ahead, even though at least part of the potential of the lunar high is lost at a maelstrom of activity. If you are working today you can be sure that the right people are looking at you and that they will be doing all they can to support both you and your plans. Finances should be strengthening now.

19 TUESDAY
Moon Age Day 6   Moon Sign Virgo

Professional developments remain generally positive and you are very convincing when you are dealing with those people around you that have influence. You may need to be just slightly careful regarding your health at the moment, because you could be more prone to minor infections than would normally be the case.

20 WEDNESDAY   *Moon Age Day 7   Moon Sign Virgo*

Conversations with others go smoothly enough at the moment and at least you are standing still for long enough to hear what they have to say in reply. There is a potentially harmonious sort of give and take between yourself and family members and this would be a great time to heal a long-standing feud.

21 THURSDAY   *Moon Age Day 8   Moon Sign Libra*

You have a strongly mercurial gift of the gab around this time and people will find you interesting to have around. Even strangers are likely to be on the receiving end of your need for conversation and you might make some new friends as a result of a different social activity. Don't rule things out today but be open to suggestion.

22 FRIDAY   *Moon Age Day 9   Moon Sign Libra*

Highly intellectual pursuits will be right up your street at the end of this working week. You should also be up for some fairly stimulating entertainment and might take yourself off to the theatre or to a concert. Getting relatives and friends to help you out with a prospective weekend project might not be as easy as you thought though.

23 SATURDAY   *Moon Age Day 10   Moon Sign Scorpio*

The domestic scene is likely to be far busier than it was even a few weeks ago. Maybe there is a lot going on in the family or it could be that you have decided to make significant changes around your home. Whatever the reason, your own four walls and the people within them are likely to occupy your thinking.

24 SUNDAY   *Moon Age Day 11   Moon Sign Scorpio*

Your imagination works overtime on this particular Sunday, which can be both a blessing and a curse. New ideas come thick and fast but you could also be faced with the idea of pitfalls that don't really exist at all. It is important to take a realistic view of life and to weight up pros and cons sensibly.

25 MONDAY *Moon Age Day 12   Moon Sign Scorpio*

Once again, all things domestic tend to be both important and fulfilling. This is not to suggest that you are ignoring the more practical, work-based area of life – though it is true that in a career sense you might be coasting for a few days. Younger people may give you good reason to be proud of them and they seem to follow your lead.

26 TUESDAY *Moon Age Day 13   Moon Sign Sagittarius*

Extremely high energy levels are pointing you towards the outside world and as a result there is something of a conflict developing within you. The way forward is to employ a sensible balance between the different things you have to do. In some ways you work best alone for the next couple of days but don't be standoffish.

27 WEDNESDAY *Moon Age Day 14   Moon Sign Sagittarius*

Relationships should be pleasant today, especially with people at home. At the same time you are now at your most romantic and can find words of love tripping from your tongue as if you were a poet. It's time to show your appreciation and you can do so in a number of both practical and frivolous ways, which are all accepted.

28 THURSDAY *Moon Age Day 15   Moon Sign Capricorn*

Armed with even more energy and enthusiasm, this is the part of the week when you are making every move count and when those around you are anxious to be on board and working alongside you. It's just that you seem to know at every stage what you should be doing and what is likely to happen. Some might call you psychic.

29 FRIDAY *Moon Age Day 16   Moon Sign Capricorn*

Don't be surprised to find setbacks and delays coming along at any time today. Changes might have to be made with regard to planned journeys and you won't be able to count on people to quite the extent you would wish. Just go with the flow and accept that everything is going to turn out fine in the end.

30 SATURDAY   *Moon Age Day 17   Moon Sign Capricorn*

Don't go ahead with anything for which you have not laid definite foundations. Your ego reappears and could get you into trouble unless you control it. Try to show everyone just how willing you are to compromise and to co-operate. If you don't do so, you could make some unnecessary enemies.

July

2018

1 SUNDAY
Moon Age Day 18   Moon Sign Aquarius

If it feels as though you have little control over your own life you can at least take heart from the fact that everyone else seems to be considering your best interests. You are not usually too happy to have others doing things for you but with the lunar low occurring at this time you will probably have very little option, at least for now.

2 MONDAY
Moon Age Day 19   Moon Sign Aquarius

The start of the week could seem fairly slow. It will take time to do things and situations are unlikely to sort themselves out as quickly as you would wish. Don't get involved in arguments or disputes that are not of your own making and take time out to smell the flowers. Money matters could be less complicated than you think.

3 TUESDAY
Moon Age Day 20   Moon Sign Pisces

This ought to be a generally favourable time for your emotional and family life. Give some time to thoughts about changes you want to make, probably in your career but don't react harshly to the plans those around you are making. Who knows, they may work more to your advantage than you would expect?

4 WEDNESDAY
Moon Age Day 21   Moon Sign Pisces

Your ideas are high-flying and quite exuberant. This means you are good to have around and you should be attracting just the right sort of influences in terms of friendship. At work you are capable, careful to get things right but at the same time keen to have fun. Leo is certainly good to know under these trends.

5 THURSDAY
Moon Age Day 22   Moon Sign Pisces

This would be a good time for hobbies or for getting involved in new interests of one sort of another. The intellectual side of your nature is definitely on display and you are able to make a good impression on all manner of people, simply by being what you naturally are. A real coup is possible at work, helped by your ready tongue.

6 FRIDAY
Moon Age Day 23   Moon Sign Aries

Business dealings should go well but you may have to be especially cautious regarding a departure you don't really understand. It is necessary to check out all facts very carefully and to avoid taking the advice of people you don't necessarily trust. In a romantic sense you are still on top form and should be making a good impression.

7 SATURDAY
Moon Age Day 24   Moon Sign Aries

It is gradually becoming apparent that your greatest joy at this time comes from your home life and probably not as a result of things that are happening beyond your own front door. You may feel slightly frustrated that you don't have everything you need to make progress in a financial sense and some extra patience will be necessary if this is the case.

8 SUNDAY
Moon Age Day 25   Moon Sign Taurus

If you have to make personal sacrifices at this time you can at least be sure that you do so for very good reasons. You will be drawn to putting in extra effort for worthy causes and can be of tremendous help to people who have less than you. Your confidence is generally high and your influence is definitely increasing.

9 MONDAY
Moon Age Day 26   Moon Sign Taurus

Put the power of your personality to good use when it comes to getting what you want. You are both attractive and deeply charismatic at this time and others can be persuaded to follow whatever course of action you decide to take. Your organisational skills are also especially good and need to be utilised.

10 TUESDAY
Moon Age Day 27   Moon Sign Gemini

You now have the chance to engage personally with a loved one. For the last few days you have probably been too busy with the practicalities of life to notice what was happening in an emotional sense. Now you can wake up to the needs others have of you and address their concerns without putting yourself out.

11 WEDNESDAY
Moon Age Day 28   Moon Sign Gemini

This is a very active period and one that makes great demands on your time and energy. Because of this you need to balance the effort with periods of relaxation. Even a little time sitting in the garden or the park now and again you can be enough. All work and no play make you both dull and tired.

12 THURSDAY
Moon Age Day 29   Moon Sign Cancer

There is now an abundance of drive and initiative and no lack of incentive to get what you want from life. Some people might think you are rather argumentative at the moment but in truth you are only going for what you know to be rightfully yours. You can't please everyone today but your loved ones will certainly be close to your heart.

13 FRIDAY
Moon Age Day 0   Moon Sign Cancer

Enjoying personal freedom should now seem much easier. You should be looking and feeling at your best at this time and you can certainly make an impression, even on people who seem to have more or less ignored you before. In financial matters you are now coming into your own and can increase your fortune as a result.

14 SATURDAY
Moon Age Day 1   Moon Sign Leo

It isn't hard to feel good about yourself when the lunar high is around, as today will demonstrate. You barely have to put in any effort in order for things to work out as you wish and people seem to be falling over themselves to lend a hand. Good fortune is on your side and when it comes to making money you are second to none.

15 SUNDAY
Moon Age Day 2   Moon Sign Leo

Personally or professionally you are at the top of your game during this part of July. Take any opportunity to make a journey and open your eyes to the masses of possibilities that are present. It is likely that you will recognise one particular chance that has been around for ages. You just didn't see it before.

16 MONDAY
Moon Age Day 3   Moon Sign Virgo

A strong sense of achievement is likely at the moment, especially when you manage to do something that has either puzzled you or defeated you in the past. Get together with friends today if you can and especially with people you don't see all that often. There are good times to be had, both with pals and with your partner.

17 TUESDAY
Moon Age Day 4   Moon Sign Virgo

This is most likely the best day of the week for dealing with all matters at home. Those closest to you should be quite approachable and will be happy to listen to almost anything you have to say. Whether or not they will be equally willing to follow your lead remains to be seen so don't expect too much.

18 WEDNESDAY
Moon Age Day 5   Moon Sign Libra

Beware of shady types at this stage of the week, and especially those who seem to be offering something for nothing. In truth nothing is what you will end up with – so you need to be scrupulous in any sort of financial dealings. Don't part with cash right now unless you are certain of what will be coming your way.

19 THURSDAY
Moon Age Day 6   Moon Sign Libra

Compromise could be your weak point today. The fact is that you know when you are correct and you won't want to give any ground at all. Leo can be rather stubborn on occasions and with the planets the way they are, that's the way you are likely to be. All the same there are times when you need to share and today is such a period.

20 FRIDAY   *Moon Age Day 7   Moon Sign Libra*

There could be a few power battles relating to who is actually in charge in a particular relationship. You don't always give ground very easily but it has to be said that you are slightly more flexible right now than would usually be the case. This doesn't mean you are being weak, merely that you are better able to find compromises.

21 SATURDAY   *Moon Age Day 8   Moon Sign Scorpio*

Pleasant conversations and a state of harmony are likely today. You can express your feelings to those closest to you but your positive disposition goes further than that because you are willing to chat to almost anyone you come across. Look out for some sound advice coming from the direction of an older colleague or a relative.

22 SUNDAY   *Moon Age Day 9   Moon Sign Scorpio*

Leisure activities enjoyed with your partner are now likely to increase and to some extent you are looking ahead more than might have been the case last week. In addition you are learning lessons from things that have gone before, so at least a small part of your mind is inclined to dwell in the past.

23 MONDAY   *Moon Age Day 10   Moon Sign Sagittarius*

One or two relationships could be turning slightly more turbulent, though this probably isn't your fault. In most situations you merely need to monitor what is going on and this probably is not the best time for too much interference. Arguments within the family should be avoided if you have any choice in the matter.

24 TUESDAY   *Moon Age Day 11   Moon Sign Sagittarius*

Opportunities to get ahead today might have something to do with romance, or at the very least could involve a co-operative venture with a loved one. You are tinged with genius right now when it comes to new ideas so listen carefully to the voice in your head. As always, you tend to act on instinct.

25 WEDNESDAY *Moon Age Day 12   Moon Sign Capricorn*

It looks as though you will be quite busy with business and practical matters today. If you are forced to stay at home because of family commitments, you should still find time to get some fresh air, even if it only in your local park. On the other hand, if you are free to do whatever you like, you might decide to embark on a journey.

26 THURSDAY *Moon Age Day 13   Moon Sign Capricorn*

Love could come knocking at your door, perhaps even if you have not been particularly looking for it at this time. You also do well in all social situations and when you are faced with having to talk in a public setting. Leo is now on top form. You love the summer and with it the chance to socialise and to move about.

27 FRIDAY *Moon Age Day 14   Moon Sign Capricorn*

Capitalise on your ability to talk to almost anyone at this time. It doesn't matter who people are, or from what background they come. You will always find something to say to them and your egalitarian nature is particularly well emphasised at this time. Once again it looks as though you would revel in the chance to travel.

28 SATURDAY *Moon Age Day 15   Moon Sign Aquarius*

You can expect a few delays while the lunar low is around but such is your optimism and enthusiasm at this time you will be able to circumnavigate any real problems quite easily. If you really want to make the most of a less than inspiring two or three days you could choose to take a break and to go somewhere really beautiful.

29 SUNDAY *Moon Age Day 16   Moon Sign Aquarius*

Get plenty of rest and don't expect to do everything yourself. Better by far right now to supervise others and to also spend a few hours planning what you intend to do later. People may be relying on you but they can get by fine just as long as you are there to offer advice. This would not be a good time for taking unnecessary financial risks.

30 MONDAY
Moon Age Day 17   Moon Sign Pisces

With some communications a little strained, you will have to work that much harder today to get your message across. It seems as though people around you are going to take offence at the slightest thing, though it has to be admitted that you may not be at your most diplomatic under present planetary trends.

31 TUESDAY
Moon Age Day 18   Moon Sign Pisces

Handling several different tasks at the same time won't be difficult for Leo today. The planets are in a strong position for you and you should also find it easier than normal to put your emotions into words. Speaking words of love is something you will do automatically and in doing so you can make those around you feel very safe and secure.

August

2018

1 WEDNESDAY ☿ *Moon Age Day 19   Moon Sign Pisces*

Avoid allowing yourself to become obsessive about situations that are not half as important as they may seem to be to you. It is important to take a longer-term view of life and to settle down a little. Leo can now be quite edgy and you won't take kindly to being instructed to do anything that goes against the grain.

2 THURSDAY ☿ *Moon Age Day 20   Moon Sign Aries*

This is certainly going to be a good time when it comes to leisure pursuits. If you can call today your own you need to be doing things that are fun, but at the same time productive in some way. Leo often finds ways and means of having both the penny and the bun but you are especially good at seeking out advantages today.

3 FRIDAY ☿ *Moon Age Day 21   Moon Sign Aries*

Some people could accuse you of being just a little too assertive, especially around your home. This can be a slight problem for Leo on occasions because you know how you want things to be and can sometimes be slightly too demanding. Make sure you take the ideas and considerations of other people on board.

4 SATURDAY ☿ *Moon Age Day 22   Moon Sign Taurus*

This will probably be the best day of the week and maybe one of the best during August to deal with career matters. You are filled with good ideas but what sets this period apart is the fact that you can convince others that your suggestions are sound. Avoid thinking about limitations and stick only to what you know is possible.

5 SUNDAY ☿ *Moon Age Day 23   Moon Sign Taurus*

It is important for you now to get yourself involved in group matters and discussions that involve numbers of people. There are times for Leo when it is best to go it alone but this is not one of them. Out of a maelstrom of ideas emanating from the talks you can pick a few winning ideas that will come to fruition later.

6 MONDAY ☿ *Moon Age Day 24   Moon Sign Gemini*

It looks as though you will be very entertaining company to have around on this particular August Monday. Try not to do too much that is constructive but instead take some time out to enjoy yourself. Even if you feel that jobs are piling up you won't really help your cause by crowding everything into today. Have a good rest.

7 TUESDAY ☿ *Moon Age Day 25   Moon Sign Gemini*

Some major professional advancement is now on the cards. It probably won't be handed to you on a plate but you are quite used to working for what you get and won't mind at all having to put in extra effort. It seems as though all the toil you have been putting in over recent weeks is now starting to pay off handsomely.

8 WEDNESDAY ☿ *Moon Age Day 26   Moon Sign Gemini*

If you are travelling you may enjoy one or two pleasant moments this week. If this is the time you have chosen to take a holiday you could not have picked a better time from an astrological point of view. Some Leos will be heavily committed to family matters at the moment and particularly involved with the needs of young people.

9 THURSDAY ☿ *Moon Age Day 27   Moon Sign Cancer*

Certain emotional impulses should now be born in mind. Don't give in to negative patterns of behaviour and try to remain as flexible as you can. Above all, recognise what is driving you at this time and spend a significant amount of time working out your own psychological imperatives and needs.

10 FRIDAY ☿ *Moon Age Day 28   Moon Sign Cancer*

With an abundance of creative energy and a good sense of what is going to work for you, today could prove to be especially successful. At the same time there is a quiet part of your nature that is trying to exert itself so take this into account too. Balance is the most important thing to cultivate now.

11 SATURDAY ☿ *Moon Age Day 0   Moon Sign Leo*

Following up on intuitive hunches is likely to work extremely well for you now and with all the power of the Moon working on your behalf you should be able to move forward successfully into new phases. Don't take friends or colleagues for granted because their ideas can work out just as well for you as for them.

12 SUNDAY ☿ *Moon Age Day 1   Moon Sign Leo*

Greater self-confidence and a determination that is off the scale are two of the legacies of the lunar high that positively overtake you at this time. There isn't much that is beyond your abilities and you can show the world just how successful Leo can be when working at its best. Take advantage of better financial prospects.

13 MONDAY ☿ *Moon Age Day 2   Moon Sign Virgo*

Socially speaking you are likely to be on top form for most of this week. It's amazing just how much you can get by mixing freely with other people. You may even get on side with those you haven't particularly liked before and that is because you are seeing aspects of their nature you haven't thought about in the past.

14 TUESDAY ☿ *Moon Age Day 3   Moon Sign Virgo*

Along comes another potential romantic highlight, with the accent on pleasure. This is August after all and if you don't take advantage of the summer while it's here you could find yourself back in the cold weather, without having taken advantage of what the season has to offer. Leave work alone, if only for a few short hours.

15 WEDNESDAY ☿   *Moon Age Day 4   Moon Sign Libra*

This is a time when you would be attracted to roaming either with your partner, family members or friends. If you are lucky enough not to be at work today you should do something quite different and enjoy the change. Not everyone is going to be on your side at present but when it matters the most people will follow your lead.

16 THURSDAY ☿   *Moon Age Day 5   Moon Sign Libra*

A short but quieter and less demanding interlude is at hand and this should give you the chance to catch up on a few things that have been put on the back burner so far this week. When dealing with younger family members try to find the time to really concentrate on what they are saying and react accordingly.

17 FRIDAY ☿   *Moon Age Day 6   Moon Sign Scorpio*

Your capacity to experience life's romantic interludes is getting greater and greater. You are also likely to be quite taken with luxuries and physical pleasures of one sort or another under prevailing trends. Leo can be either very abstemious or quite hedonistic and the latter seems to be the case now.

18 SATURDAY ☿   *Moon Age Day 7   Moon Sign Scorpio*

A surge of even greater energy should be obvious today and the sunny side of your nature is on display for everyone to see. Life ought to seem happy and fulfilling at this time and if it doesn't, you are clearly doing something wrong. Take time out to smell the flowers as you dash from one place to another.

19 SUNDAY   *Moon Age Day 8   Moon Sign Sagittarius*

It is unlikely that you can continue something in quite the same manner you did in the past. Change is part of the present planetary setup but it does tend to be of the sort that is well thought out and implemented carefully. The one thing you need to avoid for the next day or two is a tendency to throw the baby out with the bathwater.

20 MONDAY   *Moon Age Day 9   Moon Sign Sagittarius*

Today has potential, though what you might do to fully exploit it remains to be seen. In the main you will be out there enjoying yourself and this would be an ideal time to start a longer break. Do your best to please your partner and if you are looking for new love, do keep your eyes wide open right now.

21 TUESDAY   *Moon Age Day 10   Moon Sign Sagittarius*

You have a talent for nurturing and assisting others and although you sometimes keep this skill under wraps, it is more likely to show itself now than at any other time throughout the year. This makes you the champion of the underdog but also proves what a great teacher you are. Sort out a troubled friend later.

22 WEDNESDAY   *Moon Age Day 11   Moon Sign Capricorn*

Much can be achieved out here in the middle of the week if you use your energies wisely and concentrate on the task at hand. You are extremely strong willed at the moment, though of course there is nothing new about that. Despite your need to succeed do make sure that you are not trying to control other people.

23 THURSDAY   *Moon Age Day 12   Moon Sign Capricorn*

You thrive on competition at the best of times but especially so now. In sporting situations you want to win but you won't be so inclined to do so that you employ dubious strategies. It really is the case at the moment that it doesn't matter too much to you if you win or lose. It is 'how' you play the game that counts.

24 FRIDAY   *Moon Age Day 13   Moon Sign Aquarius*

Just be sure that you see the whole picture of life in a productive way before you take any prohibitive action. In reality it would be best to avoid making long-term decisions and instead you should watch and wait for a while. There is nothing to prevent you from enjoying your life on a personal and domestic level today.

25 SATURDAY   *Moon Age Day 14   Moon Sign Aquarius*

Family responsibilities may seem to get in the way of you having a good time in the way you wish. This is all part of the somewhat restricted perspective that comes with the lunar low. If you stop to think carefully there are ways and means in which you can fulfil your responsibilities towards others, whilst at the same time having fun.

26 SUNDAY   *Moon Age Day 15   Moon Sign Aquarius*

Your confidence certainly isn't lacking and you are right up there when it comes to making the best of impressions, especially on the social scene. This is not really a Sunday for trying to achieve anything material or concrete but rather for showing the world what you are capable of in terms of personality. Today you are positively scintillating.

27 MONDAY   *Moon Age Day 16   Moon Sign Pisces*

It looks as though you will be filled with nervous energy at the start of this week so there isn't much doubt that you will be on the go. You can certainly get plenty done and you are in a prime position to be of assistance to other people. At home you may be slightly restless and you need to be thinking up new little adventures.

28 TUESDAY   *Moon Age Day 17   Moon Sign Pisces*

You remain vital and enthusiastic. In short you are in the best possible position to benefit from opportunities that pass you by at breakneck speed. Such are your powers of perception at the moment that few people could fool you and no situation will be beyond your powers of reasoning. You have a zest for life that is awe-inspiring.

29 WEDNESDAY   *Moon Age Day 18   Moon Sign Aries*

You will find that others are now even more inclined to trust you than they were before. This helps your ego, though you never had any doubt about your own integrity. With this greater trust probably comes more responsibility but of a kind you should be quite happy to take on. Socialise as much as possible later in the day.

30 THURSDAY
Moon Age Day 19   Moon Sign Aries

There could be a few tricky matters developing in the professional arena, which is why you have to keep your wits about you at this stage of the week. In the main you will be responding to most situations quickly and decisively, which works well. Personal attachments cannot be treated this way because more understanding is needed.

31 FRIDAY
Moon Age Day 20   Moon Sign Aries

You tend to be carefree and easy-going for most of the time towards the end of this week, which is one of the reasons why it would be so fortunate if you happened to be on holiday at the moment. But even if you are not, you can lift the spirits of less positive people and you can light any room just by entering it.

♍ ♌ September

2018

1 SATURDAY
Moon Age Day 21   Moon Sign Taurus

This would be a great time to start a new partnership, either in business or in life. A new month means a change to some of your past attitudes and the start of September will find you anxious to progress in as many ways as you can. Be diplomatic in your approach to friends and learn what is really going on in their heads.

2 SUNDAY
Moon Age Day 22   Moon Sign Taurus

Broaden your horizons by getting as much as you can from your social life. You should also read as much as possible today because there are some words waiting for you that should be extremely inspirational. Attend to some of the little things of life and do something specifically designed to please your partner.

3 MONDAY
Moon Age Day 23   Moon Sign Gemini

People who are in a position of authority will probably be looking at you very favourably at the moment, which is why you should not waste any opportunity to make a good impression. Getting on the right side of your partner is also possible, perhaps because of some small but important gesture you are likely to make.

4 TUESDAY
Moon Age Day 24   Moon Sign Gemini

Right now it looks as though you will understand that the best sort of growth is that which starts out steadily and grows slowly. This is in direct contrast to the way your mind often works. By not rushing your fences you can make sure that every detail of situations is dealt with in advance and the progress you make will be noteworthy.

5 WEDNESDAY   *Moon Age Day 25   Moon Sign Cancer*

Expressing yourself with a great deal of conviction is not going to be at all hard and you have exactly what it takes to put your ideas across in an entertaining and yet a very constructive way. It isn't so much what you do that matters today but much more the things you are saying. Friends might be demanding but will still be charming.

6 THURSDAY   *Moon Age Day 26   Moon Sign Cancer*

Progress can now be made in all business affairs and there is a very practical feel to this part of the week. At the same time you may notice that the year is advancing and it won't be long before the weather starts to deteriorate. If there is something that needs doing out of doors, this might be the best time to tackle it.

7 FRIDAY   *Moon Age Day 27   Moon Sign Leo*

Watch out for all the new opportunities that are now surrounding you and make the very best of each and every one of them. The lunar high offers you greater control over your own destiny and allows you to take the sort of chances that might have seemed fairly reckless only a few days ago. Show the world your wilder side.

8 SATURDAY   *Moon Age Day 28   Moon Sign Leo*

This is a good period for growth and an excellent time for taking calculated risks. Yours is one of the most progressive and go-getting of all the zodiac signs and this should really be showing as the week moves on. Don't waste a single opportunity when it comes to making a favourable impression on anyone who could be important later.

9 SUNDAY   *Moon Age Day 0   Moon Sign Virgo*

This would be a really good time to take a short break or a day when you can simply have fun. You won't be taking things too seriously and should be on top form when it comes to making jokes and seeing the funny side of life. From a financial point of view it looks as though you could make some sort of small coup around now.

10 MONDAY — *Moon Age Day 1 Moon Sign Virgo*

In a professional sense this could be a somewhat challenging day, which is why it would be sensible to make sure you are prepared. People will be asking a great deal of you but that in itself is not a problem. Where slight difficulties might arise are those situations in which it is difficult to fully explain the actions you wish to take.

11 TUESDAY — *Moon Age Day 2 Moon Sign Libra*

You now become more enterprising when it comes to making financial gains. You will happily take on new responsibilities and can get jobs done in a fraction of the time it takes some of your colleagues. People are watching you closely and although you will make new allies, be careful of the odd envious type too.

12 WEDNESDAY — *Moon Age Day 3 Moon Sign Libra*

You really do have what it takes when it comes to looking ahead and planning the moves you want to make in a practical and a professional sense. At the same time you are likely to be just slightly withdrawn and more inclined than usual to think deeply about certain things. Find time to spend with family members today.

13 THURSDAY — *Moon Age Day 4 Moon Sign Scorpio*

Make time for the simpler pleasures of life, many of which pass you by because you are always so active and occupied. What is the point of making something of yourself and earning money if you never take the time out to enjoy what you have? Between now and the weekend look out for new hobbies and pastimes.

14 FRIDAY — *Moon Age Day 5 Moon Sign Scorpio*

Put fresh and innovative ideas to the test and make as much as you can out of new opportunities that are only now entering your head. Under present trends it is also possible you will be looking again at something that interested you a long time ago. New starts are more or less inevitable but even these old notions can be re-jigged.

15 SATURDAY   *Moon Age Day 6   Moon Sign Scorpio*

Today you can prove to yourself and to just about anyone how dynamic and go-getting you are. That's fine but at the same time you need to take stock of certain matters before you move on. There is always a danger that the Leo engine will run out of control and that's something to guard against for today.

16 SUNDAY   *Moon Age Day 7   Moon Sign Sagittarius*

Right now it could seem that you want to escape from some of the routines and chores that are fairly typical for a Sunday. Instead of doing what you should, try to do what you want. There's a great difference between the two, and even a few hours spent pleasing yourself will set you up for a new working week that could prove to be busy but rewarding.

17 MONDAY   *Moon Age Day 8   Moon Sign Sagittarius*

You may appear to be very much at ease today, but underneath a cool exterior you are starting to niggle about something. Ask yourself whether it would be best to take decisive action, rather than mulling things over so much. There are times for Leo when it is best to wade in and do whatever seems most appropriate straight away.

18 TUESDAY   *Moon Age Day 9   Moon Sign Capricorn*

Today should be very pleasing on the romantic front, especially for young or young-at-heart Leos. With new chances to impress someone who is important to you coming your way, there is no doubt that you should be speaking out on your own behalf. People generally should find you interesting and even fascinating now.

19 WEDNESDAY   *Moon Age Day 10   Moon Sign Capricorn*

You now appreciate minor differences between the options available to you and pinpoint your actions accordingly. Some people might even call you fussy at the moment and there may be a smile or two from friends. All the same, you do things the way you know they should be done, even if others disagree.

20 THURSDAY   *Moon Age Day 11   Moon Sign Aquarius*

The lunar low is now around and it might be slightly difficult for the moment to live up to responsibilities you know are yours. Let others take some of the strain and rely on the good offices of colleagues, friends and family members for the next couple of days. You can't be on top form all the time and some rest is good for you.

21 FRIDAY   *Moon Age Day 12   Moon Sign Aquarius*

Even though you might feel content as far as your future plans are concerned, you may still fret about matters without any just cause. That's quite natural under these trends but as long as you appreciate this, everything will turn out fine. Don't hang on to emotional memories. Let them drift away.

22 SATURDAY   *Moon Age Day 13   Moon Sign Aquarius*

A little more deliberation is called for today, though you have been in a fairly pensive frame of mind for the last few days. Stay on the right side of someone who is in charge and follow their lead rather than seeking to do what appeals specifically to you. Even if you know others are wrong there are times when it's best to keep quiet.

23 SUNDAY   *Moon Age Day 14   Moon Sign Pisces*

Your focus today is likely to be more upon having a good time than getting down to anything serious or demanding. The lunar low is out of the way but you respond to other trends that make you want to defer responsibility for another day. It would not be wise to make any major changes to your life for a day or two.

24 MONDAY   *Moon Age Day 15   Moon Sign Pisces*

Look out for a slight loss of confidence at the beginning of this week but understand that it is very temporary and is merely one legacy of a few minor planetary transits. These are not the most fortunate trends for business, mainly because your mind is likely to be elsewhere. However, if you are willing to relax, today can be fine.

25 TUESDAY   *Moon Age Day 16   Moon Sign Aries*

Travelling and meeting people ought to seem quite exciting under present trends. There are important contacts to be made, most likely with at least one individual who could become increasingly important to you later on. Friends or relatives who live at a distance might be visiting you, or else getting in touch today or in the days ahead.

26 WEDNESDAY   *Moon Age Day 17   Moon Sign Aries*

Co-operative affairs are positively highlighted at the moment, which is why today would be so good for addressing an issue to do with home or family. You remain good to know and should be in a fairly relaxed state of mind. This would also be an ideal day for travelling, maybe to somewhere you haven't been before.

27 THURSDAY   *Moon Age Day 18   Moon Sign Aries*

If you find yourself under any sort of pressure as a result of the actions of those around you, this is a time when you need to be slightly circumspect in the way you deal with matters. Leo is sometimes inclined to shoot from the hip but to do so at the moment would not be the right approach. Friends should be warm and sharing.

28 FRIDAY   *Moon Age Day 19   Moon Sign Taurus*

Intimate relationships look good and your ability to communicate with people hasn't been better all month. You just seem to find the right things to say, and at the most opportune moment. Stay away from contentious issues and don't get involved in other people's arguments. The last thing you need right now is to be over serious.

29 SATURDAY   *Moon Age Day 20   Moon Sign Taurus*

You are extremely well balanced at the moment and can take a sensible view of life, as well as being able to address issues that are troubling your friends. In romantic terms you are giving, warm and very affectionate. Even if people try to draw you into discussions or arguments at this time you won't take the bait.

30 SUNDAY
Moon Age Day 21   Moon Sign Gemini

Ideas associated with business are still quite important and although you are now likely to split your time between work and your social life, there are ways in which you can mix them successfully. Do something you want to do later in the day and leave responsibilities alone for a while, especially this evening.

October

2018

1 MONDAY
Moon Age Day 22   Moon Sign Gemini

You have a strong sense of your own ego today. That's fine because it is an important part of who you are. However, take care not to go over the top and make a few adversaries unnecessarily. Check how your ideas will have a bearing on colleagues or even friends, and then move forward cautiously.

2 TUESDAY
Moon Age Day 23   Moon Sign Cancer

Today puts the spotlight on partnerships and allows you more latitude when it comes to the influence you have on your life. You won't feel quite as restricted as may sometimes have been the case and you seem to be filled to the brim with enthusiasm. This attitude alone can go a long way but you should also be quite practical.

3 WEDNESDAY
Moon Age Day 24   Moon Sign Cancer

New friends and associates prove to be very stimulating in the middle of this working week. There is everything to play for in a business sense but even these trends are not as good as the personal possibilities that surround you. Making the best sort of impression on someone you really care about is now child's play.

4 THURSDAY
Moon Age Day 25   Moon Sign Leo

You may have the opportunity to apply new and quite revolutionary ideas to your life in a general sense. This goes much further than alterations you may wish to make at work and extends well into your personal life too. With everything to play for you are going to be slightly excitable but well able to keep control of everything.

5 FRIDAY
Moon Age Day 26   Moon Sign Leo

You are confident in your own abilities but not to a point that becomes a problem because your sense of humour is also honed to perfection. This means you are well able to laugh at yourself and your own peculiarities. One legacy of the lunar high is that you are so good to know. You are still quite excitable and perhaps need to slow down just a little.

6 SATURDAY
Moon Age Day 27   Moon Sign Virgo

Socially speaking you may find that you are not everyone's cup of tea, but why should that worry you unduly? Concentrate on the people who really like you and leave the rest alone. Life is too short and busy for you to spend countless hours trying to form relationships with people who are not your type at all.

7 SUNDAY
Moon Age Day 28   Moon Sign Virgo

Today's trends may lead you to spend time focusing intensely on the meaning of life. Your thoughts run deep – in fact so deep that they might be inaccessible to others. In the midst of working everything out you should also be taking the time to explain yourself to those around you. That way there is help on hand if you need it.

8 MONDAY
Moon Age Day 29   Moon Sign Virgo

Your finances should be improving now and you can probably afford to splash out a little on something that isn't necessary but desirable. Don't get hung up on details today, especially in your work and think about generalities rather than specifics. If there are jobs to do that are irksome, get them out of the way early.

9 TUESDAY
Moon Age Day 0   Moon Sign Libra

Fluctuations now become much more likely as far as money is concerned – a response to the present position of the smaller planets in your solar chart. Something that has been important to your life for a while could be changing and you may have to get used to a new set of circumstances. This might feed your insecurity a little.

10 WEDNESDAY   *Moon Age Day 1   Moon Sign Libra*

Understanding the motivations of others will come easier to you under present trends and you won't have any difficulty at all getting on the right side of those who are in a position to help you in one way or another. There are bound to be delays and interruptions today but you need to deal with these as patiently as you can.

11 THURSDAY   *Moon Age Day 2   Moon Sign Scorpio*

You may have to accept certain changes to your personal life, perhaps caused by the fact that others are so busy and starting new projects themselves. From a physical point of view you are likely to be on top form and you are also going to be quite competitive right now. It's a mixed bag that should lead to a busy life.

12 FRIDAY   *Moon Age Day 3   Moon Sign Scorpio*

Your ego is once again on the rise, but there's nothing especially surprising about that for people born under the zodiac sign of Leo. After a fairly prolonged period during which you could have felt somewhat restricted, you should now be on top form and raring to have a go. Don't turn down the support of people who are in the know.

13 SATURDAY   *Moon Age Day 4   Moon Sign Sagittarius*

You feel the need to change and even to revolutionise your life but this is not a process that will be possible all in a moment. The trouble is that you really do need patience today, though at a time when it is in short supply. Frustration could be the result unless you find some way to curb your anxiety and excitability.

14 SUNDAY   *Moon Age Day 5   Moon Sign Sagittarius*

Journeys, either of a mental or a physical sort, can suit you down to the ground. The year is growing older and the weather might not be all that good, but you will gain so much by being somewhere different. Travel changes your perspectives on life and that fact alone could prove to be very important as new astrological trends develop.

15 MONDAY
Moon Age Day 6   Moon Sign Capricorn

Issues of power and control are now emphasised and the new week will find you very anxious to be at the front and leading. It doesn't matter whether this is a career issue or something to do with the committee at your local village hall. You will be frustrated if you feel you are a follower under present trends.

16 TUESDAY
Moon Age Day 7   Moon Sign Capricorn

Personal satisfaction is important to you now and you seem to have the attitude that says 'If I am going to do something, I am going to do it right'. That's fine, but there could be other people around you at the moment who think slightly differently about things. You need to be both assertive and also diplomatic.

17 WEDNESDAY
Moon Age Day 8   Moon Sign Capricorn

You are not only on the go from morning until night today but will also be showing a great deal of curiosity regarding the way the world works. Keep yourself mentally busy and remain physically active but at the same time understand that you will have to stop and take stock, probably later in the day when you find moments to relax.

18 THURSDAY
Moon Age Day 9   Moon Sign Aquarius

The Moon is now in your opposite zodiac sign and the lunar low that arrives as a result will make you more withdrawn and less able to get exactly what you want from your life. In some ways it isn't all that advisable to try, especially if that means expecting even more of yourself. You may have to rely heavily on others.

19 FRIDAY
Moon Age Day 10   Moon Sign Aquarius

Expect a little conflict today between what you want for your own life and the expectations that others have of you. This is another reflection of the lunar low but fortunately by tomorrow things should seem much more settled. If you can find a quiet corner where you can be alone, then so much the better – at least for a few hours.

20 SATURDAY   *Moon Age Day 11   Moon Sign Pisces*

At this time you should see how much others are willing to defer to you, especially at home. It just appears to them that you clearly know what you are doing and that means they are willing to follow your lead. Someone in authority could also prove to be invaluable and might be inclined to back your judgement.

21 SUNDAY   *Moon Age Day 12   Moon Sign Pisces*

Twosomes and joint endeavours generally are the way forward – that is if you can get on with others well enough to achieve them. The more you co-operate today, the better things should go. Outside of work you are moving away from routines and regimes as much possible, looking instead for some variety and spontaneity.

22 MONDAY   *Moon Age Day 13   Moon Sign Pisces*

Future prospects start to look better, especially at work. Meanwhile you have the bit between your teeth regarding a prospective journey or a new project that might involve a friend. In terms of getting ahead both now and for the rest of this working week it isn't so much 'what' you know but rather 'who' you know that counts.

23 TUESDAY   *Moon Age Day 14   Moon Sign Aries*

You may have to dig deep to get at the root of a problem that has to be solved before you can progress in the way you would wish. There is always the possibility that someone close to you is not making the effort they should, so offer encouragement at every stage. Your love life should be warm and fulfilling.

24 WEDNESDAY   *Moon Age Day 15   Moon Sign Aries*

People in positions of power and influence should now seem more approachable than they would have done around this time last week. Actually, the change is not in them but in you. In conversation you can be charming at the moment and you won't have any difficulty in finding the right words to both compliment and encourage.

25 THURSDAY   *Moon Age Day 16   Moon Sign Taurus*

Communal activities tend to pep up your social life at present, bringing a breath of fresh air to situations that might have been getting rather stale in some way. Although you can't win at everything you do today, you will be making an impression and that can be very useful – if not now then at some time further down the road.

26 FRIDAY   *Moon Age Day 17   Moon Sign Taurus*

If you enjoy a challenge, as you undoubtedly do, today could leave a lasting impression and a strong feeling of achievement. Routines are definitely not for you at this time and you get on best when you can ring the changes at every opportunity. Not everyone is on your side at work but when it matters the most you do have support.

27 SATURDAY   *Moon Age Day 18   Moon Sign Gemini*

Make plenty of room in your life for freedom of expression today and make certain that you spend time in the company of other people. This is no time to be soldiering on alone or for locking yourself up in some secluded room. You can only shine when there are people to see you shining – otherwise all that effort is wasted.

28 SUNDAY   *Moon Age Day 19   Moon Sign Gemini*

Others now acknowledge your intelligence and your informed ideas. Your thinking, talking and acting are all smooth and concise and you have what it takes to instil confidence in other people, even individuals you hardly know. Even a casual conversation at a bus stop could prove useful now so keep listening.

29 MONDAY   *Moon Age Day 20   Moon Sign Cancer*

There is a strong possibility of exciting encounters taking place today and some of these come so quickly and so unexpectedly you will have to be right on the ball to make the most of them. Look towards love this week because there are pleasant times for the taking. Get to the root cause of a practical problem at home.

30 TUESDAY   *Moon Age Day 21   Moon Sign Cancer*

You feel the need to be calm and secure in your personal feelings and if anyone is upsetting you, you won't be happy. All the same it would be best to avoid arguments, even ones that have nothing much to do with you. Opt instead for taking a seat on the edge of conflicts. In personal attachments you are warm and loving.

31 WEDNESDAY   *Moon Age Day 22   Moon Sign Cancer*

Fulfilment now comes from one-to-one relationships. You may be asking yourself what the point is in being the most successful person in the world if you don't have the time to share that success with someone close to you. For Leo it is possible to achieve both, but some forethought and careful planning is required.

November
2018

1 THURSDAY
Moon Age Day 23   Moon Sign Leo

The lunar high brings new opportunities and the ability to chase a few of your dreams all the way. You may not able to use the lunar high this time for gains at work but having the Moon in your zodiac sign at this time could offer you the chance to show yourself at your best in social settings and in romantic clinches.

2 FRIDAY
Moon Age Day 24   Moon Sign Leo

It now becomes easier to achieve something of significance in your career. If you are out of work at the moment, now is the time to concentrate all your efforts because the planets lend a helping hand in your search for a job. At home you should be able to find time to impress and persuade loved ones around to your point of view.

3 SATURDAY
Moon Age Day 25   Moon Sign Virgo

You may now run into changes that force you to abandon earlier behaviour. In some ways this could be quite uncomfortable because you like to stay within your comfort zone, especially when it comes to the practical side of life. Nevertheless, the alterations that are imposed upon you will be for the best.

4 SUNDAY
Moon Age Day 26   Moon Sign Virgo

Certain people and even situations could be disappearing from your life around now but where this does happen it will generally be for the best. New friends will start to occupy an important place and some of them could come from fairly unexpected directions. Be bold when you know your future is at stake.

5 MONDAY   *Moon Age Day 27   Moon Sign Libra*

Look for a positive emphasis at work and keep on doing whatever is necessary to impress the right people. Away from your professional life it looks as though you are attracting the right sort of romantic attention and you also have what it takes to build up your resources. Having fun is likely to be generally free for now.

6 TUESDAY   *Moon Age Day 28   Moon Sign Libra*

Your sense of adventure is on the increase and it appears that nothing will be too much trouble if you think it will suit your purposes. This is a time when you could be dealing with different cultures and alternative ideas. What a great time this would be for travel. Even a short distance would alter your perspectives.

7 WEDNESDAY   *Moon Age Day 0   Moon Sign Scorpio*

Be willing to readjust your plans whenever you think it is necessary – which could be quite often under present trends. The end of the year is not far off and there may be something you feel you have not completed. Now is the time to take all your energy and to plough it into something important.

8 THURSDAY   *Moon Age Day 1   Moon Sign Scorpio*

You won't have much time to be bored today and, as has been the case for the last few days, you will prefer to keep busy. There are few limitations placed around you and although you might have to be open and honest with family members you can be diplomatic and lead people think your ideas are theirs.

9 FRIDAY   *Moon Age Day 2   Moon Sign Sagittarius*

There is a sense that you are on the brink of something very important so you need to plan your actions as carefully as you can. Don't be inclined to fire from the hip in discussions and avoid arguments as much as possible. The impression you give to others is extremely important and has far-reaching, unforeseen implications.

10 SATURDAY   *Moon Age Day 3   Moon Sign Sagittarius*

Now would be an excellent time for travel. It doesn't matter whether you intend to go five miles or five thousand miles. The important factor is that you are moving away from your usual routines and looking at something both new and different. This is something that stimulates Leo nature and brings brand new incentives.

11 SUNDAY   *Moon Age Day 4   Moon Sign Sagittarius*

You are now mentally quick and very alert. Your curiosity can be aroused by just about anything and there are gains to be made from being in the right place to seize new opportunities. You will also be extremely good at showing your best and most attractive side when it comes to social encounters.

12 MONDAY   *Moon Age Day 5   Moon Sign Capricorn*

Your sense of enterprise at work is off the scale and you have everything it takes to convince bosses and colleagues that you know the right way to move forward. It could be that you have dreamed up a way of streamlining some sort of process or that you have seen an opportunity that hasn't occurred to anyone else around you.

13 TUESDAY   *Moon Age Day 6   Moon Sign Capricorn*

You may not be quite as confident as usual, but there are still strong supporting influences around you and most things will turn out to your advantage. You may have to work harder than usual to understand what family members want of you and you will once again be involved in deep discussions, though the results should be good.

14 WEDNESDAY   *Moon Age Day 7   Moon Sign Aquarius*

Beware of acting against your better judgement and don't allow yourself to be forced into situations that are not of your own making. People may accuse you of being fairly stubborn but that's something you can live with if you get what you want in the end. Your common sense and intuition are both strong and they should guide you.

15 THURSDAY   *Moon Age Day 8   Moon Sign Aquarius*

Although you remain fairly positive, you need to take care today not to offer anything you cannot genuinely deliver. Better by far to be modest in your promises or even to let others make most of the running. This trend will not last long but you could easily come unstuck if you are too adventurous now.

16 FRIDAY   *Moon Age Day 9   Moon Sign Aquarius*

There are likely to be new opportunities today to do your own thing and travel could be high on your agenda. Don't be a stay-at-home now and make sure that you respond to any exciting offer that comes your way. The year may be getting older but the advantages are increasing. Friends should be especially encouraging now.

17 SATURDAY   ☿   *Moon Age Day 10   Moon Sign Pisces*

When it comes to general progress you are now likely to be using a great deal more ingenuity and turning your radar in the direction of quite significant alterations to your working, and maybe also your social, life. You won't take kindly to outside interference right now and tend to want to make up your own mind.

18 SUNDAY   ☿   *Moon Age Day 11   Moon Sign Pisces*

It now seems as though you may not be getting the opportunities you would wish to put across your point of view in the way you really wish to do. Make sure that the most important people are listening to what you have to say and if necessary be prepared to repeat yourself. Socially speaking you can now find contentment.

19 MONDAY   ☿   *Moon Age Day 12   Moon Sign Aries*

Getting out and about is well advised now. Winter has arrived and there could be chilly winds blowing but it is very good for you to get some fresh air and to blow away the cobwebs – more so now than usual. With everything to play for in the workplace you will really want to be on the ball.

20 TUESDAY ☿ *Moon Age Day 13   Moon Sign Aries*

Look out for positive trends in your love life bringing excitement in romance and some unexpected but positive events. Today can be really exciting, even if you don't expect it to be so as the day gets started. Respond to changes in situations, especially in relationships, and someone could develop a brand new attitude.

21 WEDNESDAY ☿ *Moon Age Day 14   Moon Sign Taurus*

Others might seem to be quite opposed to some of your ideas at the moment and you will need to persuade them carefully that you know what you are talking about. Attitude is also important when it comes to your love life. Try to be as reasonable as you can be with your partner and make sure you are really listening to them.

22 THURSDAY ☿ *Moon Age Day 15   Moon Sign Taurus*

Things should settle down nicely today, or at least they would if it were not for that Leo tendency to want personal freedom to do what you want on every level. On the one hand you are willing to watch and wait but on the other you have to keep tampering and interfering. The result could be a mixed bag.

23 FRIDAY ☿ *Moon Age Day 16   Moon Sign Taurus*

Whatever has been unsatisfactory in your life now needs sweeping away and replacing with newer and more positive actions on your part. If you can't have everything you want all at the same time, you can at least make a start. Slow and steady wins most races, but it doesn't always seem so to Leo.

24 SATURDAY ☿ *Moon Age Day 17   Moon Sign Gemini*

Home and family seems important today, probably because you feel you haven't given quite enough time to such considerations during a busy week. Attention to detail is vital when it comes to new hobbies, but there is also a very active and sporting side to your nature that positively demands your attention.

25 SUNDAY ☿ *Moon Age Day 18*   *Moon Sign Gemini*

Today's emphasis is on fun and you will be up for some real excitement and, perhaps, the chance to pit yourself against a new challenge. You seem to be in a really confident frame of mind and if there have been any minor health difficulties surrounding you of late these should now be diminished.

26 MONDAY ☿ *Moon Age Day 19*   *Moon Sign Cancer*

Your mind works like lightning, bringing new ideas even closer to reality and making you inclined towards split-second decisions. If there are jobs to do today that you don't care for, it might be best to get these out of the way as early as possible. That way you leave the decks free for more concerted action later.

27 TUESDAY ☿ *Moon Age Day 20*   *Moon Sign Cancer*

You can afford to be slightly more ambitious about plans and schemes at this stage of the week, though there is every reason to believe that your recent frenetic pace will continue for a while. For now you can take time out to look at ideas without having to implement them straight away. Some financial gains are possible.

28 WEDNESDAY ☿ *Moon Age Day 21*   *Moon Sign Leo*

Today is likely to start with a real boost as the lunar high offers you every new incentive you could wish for. Gains are likely to be evident at work but also in your social and romantic life. Whatever you decide to do today you can go for gold. When you really need some assistance now all you have to do is ask for it.

29 THURSDAY ☿ *Moon Age Day 22*   *Moon Sign Leo*

Your energy levels remain high and you won't want to sit around and wait for life to come to you today. You are filled with vitality and could easily become restless unless you keep moving and acting. You have what it takes to be all things to all people under present trends.

30 FRIDAY ☿ *Moon Age Day 23* *Moon Sign Virgo*

Now is definitely a time to act on your convictions, even if these sometimes go against the wishes or desires of those around you. On those occasions when you are absolutely certain that you are correct in your judgement, you need to act. If necessary you can explain yourself later but there may not be time to do so immediately.

December

2018

1 SATURDAY ☿ *Moon Age Day 24 Moon Sign Virgo*

Do anything and everything today that might expand your horizons. It could be the case that getting yourself up to speed this morning is slightly difficult. It's not that you are feeling lazy, more that you can't seem to latch on to the incentives you need. A little perseverance is all that is required to continue the forward progress.

2 SUNDAY ☿ *Moon Age Day 25 Moon Sign Libra*

The gentle and engaging style that you are adopting right now should prove to be a winner. All too often Leo rushes at things and on the way you don't always show others quite the level of respect you might. This certainly is not the case around now and the fact that you are so caring certainly won't be lost on colleagues and friends.

3 MONDAY ☿ *Moon Age Day 26 Moon Sign Libra*

Stand by for a little restlessness. This is something that overtakes the Lion now and again and the only way to deal with it is to keep as busy and active as possible. With family members and especially your partner you are likely to be kind and attentive. Getting stuck in a rut is certainly not for you at this time so try to keep things moving.

4 TUESDAY ☿ *Moon Age Day 27 Moon Sign Scorpio*

All business goals and incentives are now crucially important. Although the year is slowing down towards its end for some people, this certainly isn't the case for you. The chances are that you will put in more and more effort as the holidays approach, whilst at the same time taking full advantage of the social possibilities that are on offer.

5 WEDNESDAY ☿ *Moon Age Day 28   Moon Sign Scorpio*

Your everyday world is now likely to contain more than a few special moments. New faces and places bring inspiration and you seem to have exactly what it takes to turn heads wherever you go. If there is a financial matter that is worrying or frustrating you at this time, maybe you should seek some useful but impartial advice.

6 THURSDAY ☿ *Moon Age Day 29   Moon Sign Scorpio*

You can make the most of today by being expansive and very enthusiastic about future plans and goals. The rush towards Christmas has probably started around you already but you don't need to get drawn into it just yet. Leo is an inspirational and an immediate zodiac sign and you work at your best when you are spontaneous.

7 FRIDAY *Moon Age Day 0   Moon Sign Sagittarius*

What a great time this is for being involved in intellectual pursuits. The more you stretch your brain, the greater can be the rewards coming your way. Colleagues will be on your side when it matters the most and although you are beginning to become quite competitive, this is not the most important factor now.

8 SATURDAY *Moon Age Day 1   Moon Sign Sagittarius*

At this time your friends are literally your greatest asset so make sure that you are doing all you can to support them. It's worth taking some time out to be of use to a friend who has been important to you for a long time, whilst also giving some thought to entertaining family members during the forthcoming festivities.

9 SUNDAY *Moon Age Day 2   Moon Sign Capricorn*

Friends still prove to be important, as does your involvement with groups or organisations. It could be that you are involved in something that is specifically designed to help those who are less fortunate and you may also be quite physically committed today – maybe in sporting activities. Money should not be hard to come by.

10 MONDAY   *Moon Age Day 3   Moon Sign Capricorn*

This is another favourable time for broadening your horizons and it looks as though you might actually achieve something by the end of the year that you could have already given up as lost or delayed. Things can change very quickly during December and even the prospect of the holidays to come is hardly likely to get in your way.

11 TUESDAY   *Moon Age Day 4   Moon Sign Aquarius*

Don't be too cautious or sensitive in relationships today. Many Leos will be moving at such a speed this month that the lunar low will only have a marginal bearing on their lives but if you go for this approach you risk coming to a grinding halt. Use the help of others to keep situations moving.

12 WEDNESDAY   *Moon Age Day 5   Moon Sign Aquarius*

Keep going today but don't push so hard you defeat your own objectives by making yourself exhausted. What is needed right now is guile, rather than brute force. New and improved situations regarding family members and friends should be showing by the end of the day and these are likely to lift your spirits.

13 THURSDAY   *Moon Age Day 6   Moon Sign Aquarius*

Career-wise you are suited to almost any job that offers you a significant challenge, though you might be rather bored at the moment if your working life is not offering you the stimulation you would wish. In almost all situations you should be willing to take on a few confrontations if these are needed to get on.

14 FRIDAY   *Moon Age Day 7   Moon Sign Pisces*

Close emotional involvements should now prove more satisfying than ever. There are times today when you will be keen to let others know what your true feelings are and although a little patience may be necessary, you can usually get your message across. Not everyone is rooting for you at present but the people who matter the most are.

15 SATURDAY
Moon Age Day 8   Moon Sign Pisces

You could settle for a fairly quiet sort of Saturday. Planetary trends are diminished today, so you are likely to be spending moments alone, perhaps with a good book. The more you are in the company of loved ones, the greater will be your feelings of satisfaction. This might not be the best day to travel too far.

16 SUNDAY
Moon Age Day 9   Moon Sign Pisces

Make sure you are aware of the motives of others at this time, particularly those who may have some sort of interest in keeping you in the dark. Keep a high profile when you are in company and don't be put off by the sort of person who naturally tends to be pessimistic. You can be a guiding force now.

17 MONDAY
Moon Age Day 10   Moon Sign Aries

Since work matters tend to be quite progressive you can make a last push before the holidays get in your way and stop you in your tracks. If you finish the working year with a flourish it will be much easier to get going again on the other side. Make it plain when you know you are right, even if you face some opposition right now.

18 TUESDAY
Moon Age Day 11   Moon Sign Aries

It looks as though this is a period of potential financial improvement. This is obviously a positive thing so close to Christmas. Part of the situation depends upon you looking carefully at your own money, and seeing how you can rationalise some spending. In the end you should find yourself better off than you thought.

19 WEDNESDAY
Moon Age Day 12   Moon Sign Taurus

The emphasis you wish to place on material and professional plans now receives a very definite boost. Make an early start and you should find you get on top of things quickly. Routines won't satisfy you now, and instead you move forward positively into areas of life that fascinate you and which prove successful.

20 THURSDAY   *Moon Age Day 13   Moon Sign Taurus*

It isn't unusual for you, but standing out in a crowd will be quite important now as your ego needs a boost. Avoid family arguments, which cannot help you in any way at the moment, and try to take a generally optimistic view of life. Give yourself chance to relax once the daily round is over.

21 FRIDAY   *Moon Age Day 14   Moon Sign Gemini*

You should be happily on the go today and you find the possibility of any sort of travel to be quite exciting. You are now unlikely to stay in one spot and might be braving the crowds to do some last-minute Christmas shopping. A general sense of goodwill seems to pervade your life now.

22 SATURDAY   *Moon Age Day 15   Moon Sign Gemini*

Make sure you add some positive thinking to the weekend and it will tend to go with a swing. You may have to force yourself to consider Christmas, which, after all, is coming any day now. Prior planning isn't always your thing but it is necessary sometimes. Don't forget a birthday or an anniversary that is about to crop up in the family.

23 SUNDAY   *Moon Age Day 16   Moon Sign Cancer*

You are extremely self-reliant at the moment, something that at least one or two other people might find difficult to deal with. Stay away from those who seem determined to cause trouble and find the path through your own social life that fits your personal needs. Your commitment to family matters is strong.

24 MONDAY   *Moon Age Day 17   Moon Sign Cancer*

You ought to enjoy conversation greatly. Even gossip isn't beneath you on this Christmas Eve. Quality time spent with loved ones should be highly enjoyable and you may discover things about yourself that have been a mystery up to now. Make a warm and happy atmosphere for family members and friends.

25 TUESDAY
Moon Age Day 18   Moon Sign Leo

This should turn out to be a great Christmas Day for you and most situations will turn out as you might wish. Make the most of the lunar high by being proactive and determined. Rules and regulations might threaten to get in the way but you will push ahead in any case, finding ways through and round any obstacles that do come along.

26 WEDNESDAY
Moon Age Day 19   Moon Sign Leo

The pace of events at home is likely to speed up significantly and it is in the practical areas of life that you will be getting on best. Don't get involved in discussions or arguments that are pointless, mainly because you don't have the time. This would also be a really good day to get involved in some sort of travel.

27 THURSDAY
Moon Age Day 20   Moon Sign Virgo

You enjoy being amongst large groups of people and the more outrageous and busy today turns out to be, the better you will like it. Both physically and mentally you are likely to be on top form and you plough yourself into whatever is going on with a real abandon. People will enjoy simply having you around.

28 FRIDAY
Moon Age Day 21   Moon Sign Virgo

Your ability to attract the good things in life, especially money, is noteworthy now. Take whatever direction is necessary in order to get ahead, stopping short only of treading on the toes of others. Socially speaking, the kindest side of your Leo nature is now clearly on display. Open a few late presents and enjoy them.

29 SATURDAY
Moon Age Day 22   Moon Sign Libra

Avoid being too extravagant today. There is a possibility that you are spending money you don't actually have, and this could lead to a few worries at the very end of the year or into January. You should be realistic and persuade those around you to take a similar attitude. Apart from that, enjoy the fun.

30 SUNDAY   *Moon Age Day 23   Moon Sign Libra*

You can accomplish a great deal around now and won't have much difficulty finding people who want to go along with your ideas. Interrupting the flow of festivities, you now have your practical head on and may be turning your thoughts towards work, whether you are actually there or not today.

31 MONDAY   *Moon Age Day 24   Moon Sign Libra*

There should be a sense of freedom and lightness of touch predominating on this New Year's Eve. Although you may not be exactly in the mood to party until dawn, you are likely to be mixing with people you find to be very interesting, and who are distinctly interested in your ideas. Today could be quite fascinating in a number of ways.

30 SUNDAY

...

31 MONDAY

RISING SIGNS FOR LEO

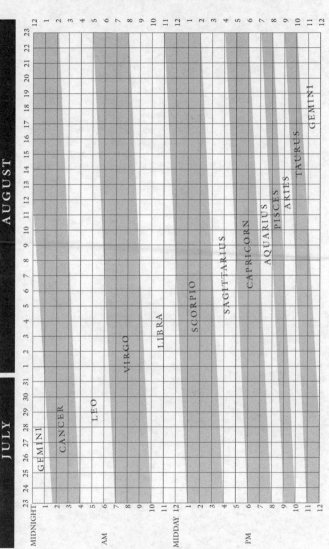

THE ZODIAC, PLANETS AND CORRESPONDENCES

The Earth revolves around the Sun once every calendar year, so when viewed from Earth the Sun appears in a different part of the sky as the year progresses. In astrology, these parts of the sky are divided into the signs of the zodiac and this means that the signs are organised in a circle. The circle begins with Aries and ends with Pisces.

Taking the zodiac sign as a starting point, astrologers then work with all the positions of planets, stars and many other factors to calculate horoscopes and birth charts and tell us what the stars have in store for us.

The table below shows the planets and Elements for each of the signs of the zodiac. Each sign belongs to one of the four Elements: Fire, Air, Earth or Water. Fire signs are creative and enthusiastic; Air signs are mentally active and thoughtful; Earth signs are constructive and practical; Water signs are emotional and have strong feelings.

It also shows the metals and gemstones associated with, or corresponding with, each sign. The correspondence is made when a metal or stone possesses properties that are held in common with a particular sign of the zodiac.

Finally, the table shows the opposite of each star sign – this is the opposite sign in the astrological circle.

Placed	Sign	Symbol	Element	Planet	Metal	Stone	Opposite
1	Aries	Ram	Fire	Mars	Iron	Bloodstone	Libra
2	Taurus	Bull	Earth	Venus	Copper	Sapphire	Scorpio
3	Gemini	Twins	Air	Mercury	Mercury	Tiger's Eye	Sagittarius
4	Cancer	Crab	Water	Moon	Silver	Pearl	Capricorn
5	Leo	Lion	Fire	Sun	Gold	Ruby	Aquarius
6	Virgo	Maiden	Earth	Mercury	Mercury	Sardonyx	Pisces
7	Libra	Scales	Air	Venus	Copper	Sapphire	Aries
8	Scorpio	Scorpion	Water	Pluto	Plutonium	Jasper	Taurus
9	Sagittarius	Archer	Fire	Jupiter	Tin	Topaz	Gemini
10	Capricorn	Goat	Earth	Saturn	Lead	Black Onyx	Cancer
11	Aquarius	Waterbearer	Air	Uranus	Uranium	Amethyst	Leo
12	Pisces	Fishes	Water	Neptune	Tin	Moonstone	Virgo